Language in Education:
Theory and Practice

INCORPORATING LITERATURE in ESL INSTRUCTION

INCORPORATING LITERATURE in ESL INSTRUCTION

Howard Sage

A publication of  Center for Applied Linguistics

Prepared by  Clearinghouse on Languages and Linguistics

PRENTICE-HALL, INC. Englewood Cliffs, NJ 07632

Library of Congress Cataloging-in-Publication Data

Sage, Howard.
  Incorporating literature in ESL instruction.

  (Language in education; 66)
  "A publication of Center of Applied Linguistics."
  Bibliography: p.
  1. English language—Study and teaching—Foreign
speakers. 2. Literature—Study and teaching.
I. ERIC Clearinghouse on Languages and Linguistics.
II. Title. III. Series.
PE1128.A2S24 1987   820'.7'1   87-7014
ISBN 0-13-455981-9

LANGUAGE IN EDUCATION: Theory and Practice 66

Office of Educational
Research and Improvement
U.S. Department of Education

This publication was prepared with funding from the Office of Educational Research and Improvement, U.S. Department of Education, under contract no. 400-86-0019. The opinions expressed in this report do not necessarily reflect the positions or policies of OERI or ED.

Editorial/production supervision: Elaine Price
Cover design: Karen Stephens
Manufacturing buyer: Margaret Rizzi

Published 1987 by Prentice-Hall, Inc.
A Division of Simon & Schuster
Englewood Cliffs, New Jersey 07632

All rights reserved. No part of this book any be
reproduced, in any form or by any means,
without permission in writing from the publisher.

Printed in the United States of America

10 9 8 7 6 5 4 3 2 1

ISBN 0-13-455981-9 01

Prentice-Hall International (UK) Limited, London
Prentice-Hall of Australia Pty. Limited, Sydney
Prentice-Hall Canada Inc., Toronto
Prentice-Hall Hispanoamericana, S.A., Mexico
Prentice-Hall of India Private Limited, New Delhi
Prentice-Hall of Japan, Inc., Tokyo
Prentice-Hall of Southeast Asia Pte. Ltd., Singapore
Editora Prentice-Hall do Brasil, Ltda., Rio de Janeiro

Language in Education:
Theory and Practice

ERIC (Educational Resources Information Center) is a nationwide network of information centers, each responsible for a given educational level or field of study. ERIC is supported by the Office of Educational Research and Improvement of the U.S. Department of Education. The basic objective of ERIC is to make current developments in educational research, instruction, and personnel preparation readily accessible to educators and members of related professions.

ERIC/CLL. The ERIC Clearinghouse on Languages and Linguistics (ERIC/CLL), one of the specialized clearinghouses in the ERIC system, is operated by the Center for Applied Linguistics (CAL). ERIC/CLL is specifically responsible for the collection and dissemination of information on research in languages and linguistics and its application to language teaching and learning.

LANGUAGE IN EDUCATION: THEORY AND PRACTICE. In addition to processing information, ERIC/CLL is also involved in information synthesis and analysis. The Clearinghouse commissions recognized authorities in languages and linguistics to write analyses of the current issues in their areas of specialty. The resultant documents, intended for use by educators and researchers, are published under the series title, Language in Education: Theory and Practice. The series includes practical guides for classroom teachers and extensive state-of-the-art papers.

This publication may be purchased directly from Prentice-Hall, Inc., Book Distribution Center, Route 59 at Brook Hill Dr., West Nyack, NY 10995, telephone (201) 767-5049. It also will be announced in the ERIC monthly abstract journal *Resources in Education (RIE)* and will be available from the ERIC Document Reproduction Service, Computer Microfilm International Corp., 3900 Wheeler Ave., Alexandria, VA 22304. See *RIE* for ordering information and ED number.

For further information on the ERIC system, ERIC/CLL, and CAL/Clearinghouse publications, write to ERIC Clearinghouse on Languages and Linguistics, Center for Applied Linguistics, 1118 22nd St. NW, Washington, DC 20037.

Gina Doggett, Editor, Language in Education

Contents

Introduction	ix
Chapter 1: The Role of Literature in ESL	1
Chapter 2: A Rationale for Using Literature in ESL	3
The Cultural Value of Literature	5
The Linguistic Importance of Literature	6
The Educational Value of Literature	7
Chapter 3: Teaching Poetry in the ESL Classroom	11
A Rationale for the Use of Poetry in ESL	11
The Main Aspects of Poetry in ESL	16
Five Major Points of Entry to a Poem	18
Principles for Teaching Poetry in the ESL Setting	23
How to Teach a Poem: A Model	26
Criteria for Choosing Poems	33
Classroom Activities During and After Discussion of a Poem	35
Chapter 4: Teaching Short Stories in the ESL Classroom	39
A Rationale for the Use of Fiction in ESL	40
The Main Aspects of Short Fiction in ESL	43
Criteria for Selecting Stories	53
Principles for Teaching Fiction in the ESL Setting	58
Classroom Activities Following Discussion of a Short Story	61
Chapter 5: The Place of Literature in the Teaching of ESL	69
Chapter 6: Guidelines for Selecting and Editing Literature for the ESL Classroom	73
References/Resources	81
References	81
Resources	89

Introduction

British poet and essayist Matthew Arnold (1822-1888), using experiences accumulated as a school inspector traveling between England and the Continent to compare British and French schools, composed the poem "Dover Beach" in 1850. In it he sought to put into words his feelings as he stood on the British shore looking at the English Channel with the French coast in the distance. "Listen," Arnold (1963) asks his imaginary or real companion, Do you hear "the grating roar/ of pebbles which the waves draw back and fling,/ At their return, up the high strand,/ begin and cease, and then again begin?" (pp. 210-211). The same "eternal note of sadness" was also heard by Sophocles (496?-406 B.C.) nearly 2,500 years earlier in another land near another body of water, the Aegean.

In alluding to Sophocles, Arnold recognizes the timelessness and universality of human experience. Sophocles, he suggests, also felt and understood human suffering. The two shared at least one additional attribute: They both sought to put their feelings into words. For both, spanning the distance from experiencing life to writing about it was natural; for them, language was an integral part of life. Both Arnold, the British school inspector and Sophocles, the Greek dramatist, although they lived thousands of years and miles apart, shared the love of and need to express their feelings in literary language.

Literary language, Balakian (1977) emphasizes, like most kinds of language, bridges "the subjective state and the physical reality of the outside world." It serves as an excellent model for observing and studying as one learns a language. "The teacher of languages is at the same time a teacher of literature, and the teacher of literature is a teacher of language, for the two functions are inseparable; they are communicating vessels that nourish each other, they constantly invade each other's territory and cannot be conceived except as a single reality" (p. 5). Allen (1978) describes the interaction as follows: "If human experience is the *what* of literature, then surely language is part of the *how*" (p. 326).

Literary language presents the universality of human experience and stimulates readers to be continually renewed by their experience, by what Wordsworth, as recast by Thomas Wolfe (1957), called "the music of the lost world . . . the great forgotten language, the lost faces, the stone, the leaf, the door" (p. 503).

1
The Role of Literature in ESL

Literature takes on varied, sometimes seemingly conflicting faces in the world of English as a second language (ESL). While literary language is helpful for learning a language, its more important purpose is "the revelation of creativity, of the knowledge of the self and of others manifested by that language used in literary context" (Balakian, 1977, p. 4). Language teachers, according to Balakian, often misconstrue literary language as communication rather than as creation. As a result, in foreign and second language classrooms, literature may serve mundane rather than creative gods.

This liability is familiar to both the proponents and opponents of literature in ESL. As the result of various trends, literature--at least creative uses of literature--has been pushed to the back of or even completely out of many classrooms. Nevertheless, literature has continued to be widely used in its pure forms and in various adaptations in ESL teaching. It would be difficult, for one thing, to drive any method completely out. Literature reemerges in other guises, such as in dialogues, in songs, and in other forms in ESL texts. Wolfson's (1979) study of spoken narration provides an example of an oral form that is of great relevance to literature in ESL.

Although literature, as a part of ESL, has suffered both from attacks by ESL people and concerted attempts by some to disregard it, it has never been ignored.

The controversy--if there is a controversy--centers not on whether literature should or should not be a part of ESL curriculums, but on how, when, where, and why it should be used. Nothing could be healthier for literature and for ESL teaching than this debate. Vigorous discussion of how literature and ESL instruction can work together and interact for the benefit of students and teachers has resulted in and continues to promise interesting ideas, learning, and improved instruction for all. The controversy reflects a natural interest in and excitement about literature itself and its place in ESL instruction. Fortunately, it has attracted some of the best minds. These teachers continue to find the use of literature in language teaching an interesting and worthy concern.

2
A Rationale for the Use of Literature in ESL

"The disregard of literature is widespread and misguided." It creates "a condition of exile rather than providing a new homeland" (Charlesworth, 1978, p. 157). The reasons for the disregard of literature in the ESL curriculum are outside the domain of this volume. Instead, the many excellent reasons for incorporating literature in the curriculum are discussed here.

Literature is inherently human; its stories, poems, and plays portray a wide variety of human concerns and needs. Because it reflects people's timeless values and preoccupations, literature attracts readers. Of course, these universal concerns take on individual guises from work to work. David Copperfield, for example, roams the special environment of London's Inner Temple and courts Agnes in the shadows of Canterbury Cathedral in a particular British Victorian manner, while Eudora Welty's American musician, Powerhouse, from the story of the same name, tramps the Mississippi Delta and announces his loneliness in an idiom and a way that American Southerners can best comprehend. Yet both accounts describe pleasures and plights that are familiar to all human beings. The perennial concerns of the heroes and heroines depicted in these fictions, if presented appropriately, communicate to all. The works discussed here amply demonstrate literature's inherent humanity.

At its best, literature depicts situations, people, and impulses that most people can recognize, consciously or unconsciously, as true, even when they cannot or will not identify with them. Literature strives for universality. Even when presenting an account or a feeling that a reader may not or cannot experience, it brings out what in the action or feeling is common to many people. The experience may appeal to so many varied imaginations that it can claim universality.

Munro (1969) cites as a reason for teaching English literature abroad that it reflects the human condition better than other literatures. But natives of all countries probably feel that their literature better reflects the human condition than all others. Fairer and closer to the truth may be the notion that all literature--Korean, Peruvian, or English--reflects the human condition.

Human beings have always faced uncertainties and loneliness as well as fulfillment, and writers from William Blake to Samuel Beckett have depicted both sides of life. Literature is rooted in daily life, the activities that people carry out each day. The world of ordering food and drink, catching buses and trains, and making and breaking appointments runs through all literature. And, of course, it is a world that ESL students must become familiar with. Literature can help students become comfortable and functional in their new environment. Beneath the surface reality, of course, exists the soul of a society, and a student, as Bradford (1968) suggests, can learn to understand not only the top layers but also underlying psychological elements.

Literature's universality includes not only people and events but extends also to issues. Certain problems have always puzzled people, and significant ideas have always been intriguing. Arnold's wish to have communicated more fully with a person no longer available, also expressed by Hayden in "Those Winter Sundays" (discussed in Chapter 3), seems to occur in the work of some writers in all times.

In addition, literature attempts to provide clarity. Literature, writes Povey (1967), makes people aware and brings them insight. Literature attempts to unravel, often at the price of great turmoil and suffering to author, characters, and readers, the most intricate and delicate of tensions. It releases what it must release in the quest for truth.

Can literature change people? Moody (1971) says literature makes four major contributions to learning, including especially personal development. Literature, he argues, can train people's sensory, intellectual, affective, social, and perhaps religious faculties. It can also help develop a person's character and moral judgment.

Of course the primary lure of literature, and the major value of literature to ESL students, is its cultural content:

> It seems safe enough to assert that English literature would make a valuable transitional material. Literature gives evidence of the widest variety of syntax, the richest variations of vocabulary discrimination. It provides examples of the language employed at its most effective, subtle, and suggestive. As literature sets out the potential

of the English language it serves as an encouragement, guide, target to the presently limited linguistic achievement of the foreign student. (Povey, 1979, p. 162)

The Cultural Value of Literature

ESL students require more than language instruction; they also need an orientation to the target culture. This culture is at best somewhat unfamiliar, and often completely unknown to these students. Teachers and administrators who have struggled with this difficulty have always found a solution in the cultural values inherent in and transmitted through literature.

Because literature provides a model of a culture, it is "one of the most obvious and valuable means of attaining cultural insights" (Scott, 1964, p. 490). This function, Scott suggests, should be stressed by ESL programs. Scott is not alone in his advocacy of literature as an effective vehicle of cultural learning. Literature, writes Rosenblatt (1978), empowers the reader to overcome the limitations of sex, race, or culture. Povey (1979) adds that "literature is a link towards that culture which sustains the expression of any language" (p. 42). Marshall (1979) found that she herself could better appreciate students' cultural background when she helped them conquer the barriers they encountered when reading literature from outside their culture.

McKay (1982) points out that the cultural problems found in teaching literature are not all necessarily to be avoided. Kujoory (1978), paraphrasing Tuers (1971) concerning John Updike's short story, "A & P," says that Iranian students had difficulty with the story because the generation gap is "less astringent" (pp. 223-224) in Iran than in the United States. Students benefit from dealing with such problems because by surmounting cross-cultural barriers, they develop their own creativity. Marshall (1979), for example, remarks that Puerto Rican students are often weak in monosyllabic, Anglo-Saxon words but are strong in their knowledge and use of Latinate vocabulary, as well as syntax. Thus these speakers are at an advantage, even compared with native-English-speaking people, when they try to understand the mind and language of a poet such as Milton; the strength thus compensates for the first weakness. Literature both overcomes many barriers between cultures and exposes them so that readers may become more responsive to them and improve their communication across cultures.

The Linguistic Importance of Literature

Ultimately ESL teachers must determine the linguistic benefits of studying literature in an ESL context. The rewards are significant and numerous. Literature in English is English at its best. Lee (1970) crystallizes this argument in his editorial:

> It is in literature that the resources of the language are most fully and skillfully used. It seems to follow that literature should enter into the language study of those who are to use the language with the greatest possible skill and effect. (pp. 1-2)

Even the loudest detractors and severest critics of the use of literature in an ESL context, such as Blatchford (1972, 1974), never state that literature is anything but the highest use to which the language can be put. They deny only its utility for ESL students.

This noble view of literature as the manifestation of language resources used as fully and as skillfully as possible does not conflict with the concept of literature's usefulness. In fact, as Widdowson (1975) defines literature, its outstanding value is precisely in its being related to but distinct from conventional uses of language. While it may share many of the characteristics and purposes of conventional language, literary language does not depend on conventional grammar or external context (that is, outside the work) for its meaning, a point to be elaborated later. The ESL student who grasps this characteristic of literary language will have learned much about the various uses to which English, literary and conventional, is put and will ultimately be able to use them himself or herself.

Even before achieving such advanced understanding, the nonnative reader can benefit in other ways from literature. Literature models a wide range of communicative strategies. Through literature, sooner or later, the student encounters nearly every kind of communicative technique speakers use or think of using. Literature displays a broader range of such communication strategies than any other single ESL teaching component. Moreover, it is a teaching aid for all language skills, extending, as Povey (1967) writes, "linguistic knowledge by giving evidence of extensive and subtle vocabulary usage and complex and exact syntax" (p. 42). It stimulates and improves a student's listening ability when used aurally and encourages oral practice through discussion, as well as offering many interesting chances to write

(Moody, 1971). In short, it extends linguistic knowledge, affirms McKay (1982), on the levels of usage and use (*usage* refers to knowledge of linguistic rules; *use* to understanding how to apply the rules effectively in actual communication exchanges). As Marquardt (1968) observes, "the study of the literature of the language is felt to be the surest way to attain these more elusive qualities that go to make up a total mastery of the language" (p. 8). It has in sum, the broadest utility imaginable.

Still, critics of using literature in ESL instruction, like Blatchford (1972, 1974), have made arguments based on (a) the objectives stated by administrators and teachers in English language programs in each country; (b) the trend in the profession toward sociolinguistic uses of language and communicative competence; and (c) inadequate training of teachers in literary studies. Of the three arguments, only the latter, the need to help teachers to teach literature more effectively, makes sense. The others are based, as Blatchford acknowledges, on local and temporal concerns. These issues must surely be raised, but after they are considered and dealt with, as they easily can be, literature will show itself to be flexible enough to adapt to any considerations of time and place, and resume its rightful position as the best--at once the richest and the most useful--resource available to language teachers and their students.

The Educational Value of Literature

No rationale for the study of literature would stand up if it did not consider literature's effects on learning. Does literature, in fact, contribute to learning, not just language learning but all kinds of learning? The question has been fully discussed by both proponents and opponents of literature in ESL curricula. Widdowson (1982), countering the critics who advocate only the so-called practical uses of language, replies that life entails more than achieving utilitarian tasks such as ordering food. He and other scholars agree that literature should have an educational purpose in the broadest sense, not merly a utilitarian function.

Adeyanju (1978) laments that as ESL has come to be associated with skills development, literature seems to have been left behind. Summarizing Blatchford, Marckwardt (1978) acknowledges a reluctance to open the doors of literature study to students who will have only limited exposure to English. Yet he agrees with Kintanar (1972) that a language's literature must be studied, for without it, the language itself would be different. Language study, asserts Kintanar, is incomplete without literature study. Thus literature has a "justifiable and profitable place ... in the English curriculum, irrespective of the role of the English language within the country, although it will differ in nature as the role of the language differs" (Marckwardt, 1978, p. 19). That role should have a great deal to do with learning. Yet it has often been subordinated to--or some have limited it to--the acquisition of skills. DiPietro (1982) suggests this imbalance results from the fact that "we EFL teachers are a pragmatic lot." If skill attainment is not the goal of a class activity, he suggests, teachers consider it without value (p. 216). Yet other kinds of knowledge can and should be gained from literature.

Literature provides much besides knowledge of basic language skills. By modeling language, literature teaches sustained, significant communication. ESL is more than just a matter of gaining mastery of many isolated communicative situations such as renting an apartment or making a bank deposit (DiPietro, 1982). Literature, in short, models and teaches coherence of language and thought.

Obviously, it is the instructor's task when using literature with ESL students to teach it as sustained, significant communication. Yet many teachers consider the task too difficult and too frightening even to begin. They are invariably certain they could never complete it. Yet these same teachers can often teach difficult expository essays with great sensitivity. Literature may indeed, at first, confuse and overwhelm teachers who are inexperienced with it. Unless the teacher is confident and secure, even the best rationale for using literature with nonnative readers is meaningless. Happily, ESL teachers have available a painless and easily comprehensible way to handle and conquer their fears.

Teaching literature to foreign students does not require knowing all the answers. What is required instead is the ability to raise and inspire questions about the literature. The teacher is a facilitator who first carefully reads and enjoys the literature. The facilitator should then raise questions with the students. No question is too trivial or too silly. The questions may be factual (e.g., *Is there an actual date or real person in the work?*), esthetic (e.g., *What do I like in this work and why?*), or critical (e.g., *What seems most useful or most memorable in the work?*). There is no limit to the number or type of questions. There is no need to answer the questions definitively; they should simply be raised and discussed. Put forth your thoughts. Listen to theirs. The students will appreciate your courage and honesty and will soon follow your lead in questioning.

The next time you think about teaching literature, and start to recoil from the work, be brave. Ask a question; then another, and another. You have begun to teach literature. This basic question-asking technique will be explored in this volume with specific poems and stories.

Inherent in literature is its function of conveying knowledge. It can transmit the knowledge of any discipline, including chemistry, history, or sociology (Moody, 1971). Moody sketched some of the vast areas of knowledge available through literature, but even his list is only partial. Knowledge of all sorts, past and present, is available through literature.

The knowledge literature transmits is not, of course, limited to factual information or theories. Literature may posit or depict something that has not, up to the moment of the story, poem, play, or novel, been conceived of, or, if it has been envisioned, has not yet been fully understood. It presents instead, as Widdowson (1983) observes, a "new reality" (p. 31). That is, the reader is not expected to understand a passage within a conventional or previously erected frame of reference. A situation, feeling, or action conveyed in a work often depends on no outside context for its validity. Its "reality" is based only on its assertion and existence in the work itself. In this way, literature differs from other kinds of discourse. For example, a question such as *Would you tell me how to get to 6 Belsize Crescent, N.W. 3?* assumes that such an address exists in a particular town, and the questioner wishes to know how to get there. This may not be true of some literary discourse. Literature often requires the reader to interpret it without the benefit of such guides or definite laws but in terms of new insights or information given for the first time exclusively by the writer. This requirement gives the reader an opportunity to experience a unique kind of discourse, which Widdowson rightly asserts many readers would embrace. Literature, conceived of in this way, can contribute "to both the process and purpose of learning" (Widdowson, 1982, p. 214)--not only language learning, but all learning.

3
Teaching Poetry in the ESL Classroom

Many ESL instructors, curriculum developers, administrators, and researchers support the use of literature for ESL students. They enjoy researching it, teaching it, and having it in their programs. However, when asked to teach or oversee the teaching of poetry, those who are usually confident of success in teaching literature experience an age-old and primitive squeamishness. Faced with poetry, they remember frighteningly incomprehensible high school poetry class sessions and begin to wonder if the literature-and-ESL combination is a good idea after all. Meeting and reading poetry again, after perhaps many years, and teaching it to ESL students, is not only a good idea but can give the teacher a fresh opportunity to enjoy and understand poetry--a genre that invites involvement, enjoyment, and understanding in a new situation.

Poetry--its teaching, studying, reading, and writing--needs no defense, although it has been successfully defended over the centuries by the likes of Sir Philip Sidney (1554-1586), Samuel Taylor Coleridge (1772-1834), and T.S. Eliot (1888-1965), among others. More important, poetry demonstrates its own significance. The assumption that poetry is difficult, and that it is the last subject we should teach, is just that--an unfounded assumption. Many factors--various fears and bad experiences--have led to the formation of this assumption. They are real, yet the positive points about poetry far outweigh the obstacles. They can be arranged into five main categories of benefits: (a) educational and learning; (b) emotional; (c) cultural; (d) linguistic; and (e) esthetic.

A Rationale for the Use of Poetry in ESL

Poetry can contribute to the learning and teaching of basic language skills. However, these skills have not been recognized as basic (Charlesworth, 1978). The most significant connection between learning and poetry is metaphor. Most learning, as Charlesworth points out, takes place through a metaphorical process, relating the unfamiliar to what the student already knows. Since most poetry consciously or unconsciously uses metaphor as one of its primary methods, poetry offers a significant learning process. More concretely, in a study of writing students in Ghana described by Watts (1981), their grammar errors, especially errors of tense and countable and uncountable forms, began to disappear as a result of their experience with poetry.

What kind of poetry is most useful for ESL students? Teachers commonly assume that simple poetry is best, but they may be wrong. Students tend to be bored by overly simple poetry: "It was found that readers derive initial pleasure from a poem they understand and like but they also derive pleasure from understanding a poem that is too difficult to have prompted pleasure from the initial reading" (Charlesworth, 1978, p. 160). Thus students benefit when they try to grasp more challenging poems.

At least two additional learning benefits can be derived from studying poetry. The first is the appreciation of the writer's composition process, which students gain by studying poems by components. Once they see each part clearly, students can consider how the poet put the poem together. They do not learn to write their own poetry this way; rather, having isolated and grasped each component of a poem, they are led to an appreciation of how the poet made all the poem's components fuse into a whole. In this way, the student is able to comprehend the poet's composition process. The student is in a position to imagine the movement from first draft to revision. A corollary benefit is that the student has in fact increased his or her insight into language. Thus the student develops sensitivity for words and discoveries that may later grow into a deeper interest and greater analytical ability (Spuler, 1981). Spuler also states that poetry, taught at the earliest possible time, can establish a basis for a better understanding of literature later in the student's education. The openness required to interpret a poem--as there is no absolute right in a poem (Charlesworth, 1978)--in itself provides a rare learning benefit.

Wallace Stevens (1879-1955), a contemporary American poet, called it "the malady of the quotidian" (p. 59) in his poem "The Man Whose Pharynx Was Bad" (1959). He was referring to the weight of daily life, which seems to compel people to repeat activities day after day without variation. Yet Stevens and other poets have shown that the ordinary moments are a proper and even fertile source of poetic inspiration. Such moments, when transformed into poetry, stimulate feelings. Poets lead readers to fuller experiences, not only of ordinary moments, but also special moments. Poetry uses language to evoke and exalt special qualities of life, and suffuses readers with feelings.

In addition to the ordinary and the special moments, life offers the unexpected. Poetry frequently depicts the pleasure of such moments. Although this aspect of life is often ignored in education, when it occurs in rhyme, rhythm, or words, it delights (Charlesworth, 1978). Readers are reached on both the intellectual and the emotional level. Surprise in poetry offers the experience of pure, undiluted pleasure--heightened because the reader neither asked for nor expected it.

Poetry, especially lyric poetry, which focuses on feelings, provides still another emotional benefit. It affords the opportunity to observe and encounter writers as they are expressing themselves most intensely. Lyric poems--perhaps all poems--are written at moments when the poet is so full of feelings that he or she must express them or burst. Such a poem allows the reader to look on as the poet releases this emotion. As in all such heightened moments, people are often moved to self-expression of emotions, in words or tears, or silence. Feelings are aroused in harmony with the poet's own. The reader's emotional response is to some the ultimate and healthiest benefit of poetry.

Almost every medium transmits culture. Poetry has always been one of the most delicate and fecund transmitters of culture. Charlesworth (1978) says poetry is a major manifestation of culture. William Marquardt (1968) shows what poetry about foreign cultures by Americans reveals about Americans' ability to relate to and accept foreign cultures. The transmission of culture through poetry is evidenced by the well-known untranslatability of most poems from one language to another. Poems, in most cases, cannot be effectively translated because they are too steeped in their own culture. They cannot be transported elsewhere without loss of identity.

This benefit of poetry is simultaneously one of the most difficult challenges confronting ESL teachers. The poem contains so many cultural elements--allusions, vocabulary, idioms, tone-- that do not translate easily or at all. Such material may discourage or even repel students and complicate the teacher's task. Glosses, if they are done well, provide the necessary information. At the same time, glosses may be distracting or, worse, discouraging, if they are too numerous. Bad glosses can even mislead students. A more positive approach, that of encouraging students to discover the cultural knowledge they require to understand a poem, is discussed later in this chapter.

Poetry is a language experience. The manifestations of language common to poetry are so numerous and so diverse that we can call them languages--that is, words and sentences used to express a variety of states of mind. Figurative language, for example, includes metaphor, simile, symbolism, paradox, personification, and irony. According to Widdowson (1982), poetry serves functions as useful as those served by conversation. Poetry is not the limited or arcane brand of language many suppose it to be. It adapts itself to a myriad of human uses. Widdowson (1982) shows how poetry makes the so-called practical functions of recent linguistic texts apear ethereal.

The sounds of poetry serve practical purposes. Poets such as Robert Frost, Emily Dickinson, Walt Whitman, and Theodore Roethke, for example, use rhythmic patterns that strongly reinforce American English intonation (Marquardt, 1968). Their poems can be used even for pronunciation drills, if desired. Onomatopoeia, alliteration, and other sound phenomena common to poetry may reach the nonnative ear more rapidly than nonpoetical sounds. The music of poetry is one of its supreme benefits.

In addition to the musical pleasure and value derived from poetic language, poetry is a fertile source of figurative language (Spinelli & Williams, 1981). The language of poetry "manifests its power and flexibility far beyond the writing and speech of everyday use" (Charlesworth, 1978, p. 162); it is exemplary language. McConochie and Sage (1985) illustrate how poetry represents the ultimate use of the language. In short, poetry is language in its most economical and compressed form. Nowottny (1965) says poetry is "language at full stretch" (p. 5).

When language is stretched to possibly its ultimate use, it becomes a special language. It evokes the same responses evoked by anything different: that is, unusual, difficult, or even radical. Poetry has a unique license to devise its own syntactical rules without being considered incorrect. Certainly, poetry does so more than prose, though this has not been scientifically measured. Several attempts have been made to compare poetry and nonpoetic prose on this aspect (Perrine, 1982; Widdowson, 1975).

Fear that such "radical" language may be too difficult, as well as concern about its incorrectness, underlies most pedagogic objections to it. In the ESL context, this has led some teachers to declare poetry off-limits. The lengthy and complex arguments over the general question of poetry's appropriateness for ESL students have already been documented. For now, it is enough to urge that ESL teaching be flexible enough for students to learn language from both conventional and poetic modes of discourse. Is this *enfant terrible*, poetic language, good for ESL students' language learning? Do students learn more effectively from nonpoetic language? No compelling evidence proves this to be the case, and a good many have espoused the benefits of poetic language in the teaching of English to nonnative learners.

Without poetry, in fact, perhaps knowledge about language would be diminished. Poetry has served to codify language, to record it in a form that preserves for future reference the use of language as it is at a given time, and thus provides a stable basis for rereading, refining, and changing it (McConochie, 1979). McConochie names the *Iliad*, the *Odyssey*, and *El Cid* in Spanish as just a few of the examples of this function of poetry.

McConochie (1982) states moreover that poetry is so essential to the study of English that, without it, students' English language diet is incomplete. That is, without poetry, they cannot gain a full grasp of the quality of English. Their language diet would be nutritionally deficient. Poetry is neither additive nor a side dish; it is a staple on the menu for learning English.

Once the centrality of poetry to the learning of English is acknowledged, the great learning benefit offered by poetry itself--the quality of poetry--can be appreciated. What is poetry? A primary characteristic discussed by Charlesworth (1978) and many others is that poetry is universal. It is not limited to a single race, country, or religion. One among many explanations for poetry's universality is simply that its dramatic nature makes it universally compelling. All poems are universal dramas, says McConochie (1979), alluding to work by Brooks and Warren (1960), that pervade all people's lives.

Widdowson (1975) offers a useful guide for discovering and defining the essence of poetry. His suggestions stem, at least initially, from a linguistic point of view. He observes that each poem creates its own language or dialect, necessitating a unique grammar. The grammar of each poem is sufficiently different from conventional grammar to require its own grammatical rules, and cannot always be understood with reference to the standard grammar. The literary work is a "separate and self-contained whole" (p. 36), and the typical phonological, syntactical, or semantic code of the language does not determine the poem's sounds, structure, or meaning. (Of course, such uniqueness does not automatically make a text literary.) Poetry is linguistically unique because it uses language structures that go beyond those normally enforced by linguistic rules. These structures impart meaning to each language component (verbs, articles, etc.), and the conventional linguistic value of these components adds to their special semantic value.

Widdowson (1975) also distinguishes literature from its social context: "Literary discourse is independent of normal interaction, has no links with any preceding discourse and anticipates no subsequent activity, either verbal or otherwise" (p. 54). This statement is true of many literary works. To be understood, literature must use patterns. It must substitute its own code for the conventional one. Widdowson (1975) illustrates this point with selected poetic texts. Widdowson's treatment of the linguistic uniqueness of poetry is of great importance and should be consulted in its entirety.

Widdowson's discussion of the distinguishing features of written literature is crucial to understanding the nature of poetry itself. Poetry combines in its own special way the characteristics of both spoken and written modes. Poetry, perhaps all literature, as Widdowson suggests, "appears to be a mode of communicating which has no analogue in conventional uses of language" (p. 64). While his discussion cannot settle the question of the essential nature of poetry, it does provide some insight into the many benefits that poetry in and of itself offers. It also points the way for ESL professionals in particular to uncover aspects and principles of successfully studying and teaching poetry.

The Main Aspects of Poetry in ESL

When ESL teachers address a poem with the necessity or goal of presenting the experience to students, what sort of meeting is it? A poem is a poet's attempt to record an experience or state a feeling the poet has understood to some extent. A finished poem--finished in the sense of having received the final, careful attention of the poet--embodies in its words, sentences, and form the poet's meaning to the extent that the poet succeeds in grasping and expressing it. If it has been successfully composed, it acts as a whole, concealing its craft. The poet's choice of one word over another, the selection of one formal approach instead of some other, and similar evidence of artistic decisions are not apparent. It is met and read in its final stage, a linguistic and formal embodiment of an experience or feeling.

Encountering a poem in its finished state, teachers and readers may feel overwhelmed. It may seem difficult to know how or even where to begin in order to understand it, even on the literal level. Poetry, especially well-crafted poetry, may appear to conceal its craft so well that the reader may feel it is difficult or even impossible to penetrate it sufficiently to understand it. When the poem must be absorbed within a limited time period, a reader or teacher may initially find it so difficult to make sense of it that he or she may abandon the effort. A poem may appear to be so self-contained that it discourages readers from entering.

Such discouragement may take two forms. The reader may find that the poem holds together so well that to probe its manner of construction seems to be a destructive act. The reader is reluctant to "tear the poem apart," as this feeling is sometimes expressed. Or a reader may view the poem as so compact that it is difficult to distinguish one aspect of the poem from another. The elements that make up the poem may simply seem impossible to isolate.

The first difficulty is expressed so often and so intensely that it deserves an immediate and direct response. It is true that to understand a poem a reader may need to temporarily disentangle one section from another, one voice from another voice, one line, one word, one sound from other lines, words, and sounds. However, no destructive intent or action is at work here. The exercise is inherently creative: at each stage of the disentanglement, the reader strives to grasp how the poet fused disparate elements and brought conflicting forces into a harmonious whole.

Both kinds of reader reluctance are calls for help. New readers need help knowing where to begin, which aspects to approach first in the task of understanding a poem. The pertinent questions are as follows: What aspects of a poem are significant enough to provide an initial grasp of the poem? What aspects of the poem yield the greatest benefits in understanding? What aspects of a poem have traditionally most helped a reader gain entrance to it?

Contrary to many readers' fears, poets do not wish to conceal their feelings or experiences. They wish to reveal and share them. Consciously or unconsciously, a poet displays his or her words, patterns, feelings, ideas, voices, and visions of life on a page for all to see and hear. While he or she may not know or even care whether anyone actually reads them, the poems are there to be seen and seen again, heard and reheard. A poem and all its parts continually invite readers to enter. Yet the best openings for the reader are not immediately apparent.

A poem by Wallace Stevens (1879-1955) entitled "Thirteen Ways of Looking at a Blackbird" offers the chance to compare different impressions of a natural element and to consider the various associations a blackbird evokes. Robert Frost's (1874-1963) "Stopping by Woods on a Snowy Evening" provides another kind of opportunity. Entry to the poem is enabled by questions of identification and motivation: Who is stopping? Who owns the woods? Why would someone risk freezing to death by lingering in the frozen woods on an especially dark night? Such obvious questions are spontaneous, and the reader has no immediate need to look further. Not every poem provides the same opportunity or degree of accessibility; poems have varying accessibility ratios. But all poems can be approached from many directions. Not all apertures reveal as much about a poem as quickly as some, but all are useful and none lead the reader completely astray.

After entering at one point, the reader will quickly arrive at other crucial locations. Each pressure point is connected, as in Chinese acupuncture, to others, perhaps far removed. The reader gains new information at each point and finds new routes to still other new points of information and departure. Each location is a source of meaning that intersects with other criss-crossing lines of meaning. A poem is an intersection of infinite networks, all interweaving and revealing themselves finally as a whole. The crucial paradox of poetry is that the more diverse its signals, the more they are one.

Five Major Points of Entry to a Poem

While nearly all explorations of a poem will bring some understanding, certain starting points have proven especially useful for retracing the poet's clear tracks. Any analysis of a poem achieves some understanding of the poet and the poem by tracing or retracing the poet's steps. Ths process does not differ greatly from methods used to grasp any account of an experience or expression of feelings--or in understanding an experience itself. The analyst needs to know what, if anything, happened; who was involved; the sequence in which it occurred or is perceived to have occurred; the sensory environment (sounds, sights, smells, tastes, etc.); and, if possible, what it amounts to--what, in short, it means. While other starting points, such as tone, mythological basis, sentence structure, and so on, may be revealing and even at times essential or predominant, these five points usually involve the greatest number of and the most important interconnections; they go most directly to the poem's center.

A 26-word, four-line poem of the 14th century, "Western Wind," incorporates the anonymous poet's feelings in two stanzas that use all five basic poetic aspects. Adapted for the Taverner *Mass* written by Thomas Taverner (1490-1545/46), "Western Wind" is a tapestry of narration, speaking voice, form, language, and theme.

> Western wind, when wilt thou blow,
> The small rain down can rain?
> Christ, if my love were in my arms,
> And I in my bed again!

This poem may be approached from several directions. The clearest starting point is to determine what is happening in the poem. Although the question may seem naive, it can be expected to elicit many suggestions. A boat is lost at sea, one student may postulate. Another may suggest that someone is in jail. A third may posit that a man or woman is praying for rain during a dry spell. If students do not suggest where the events may be taking place, the question of location may be interjected. Then the two questions may be played off against each other, eliciting reactions while encouraging the students to relate the two sets of answers. The teacher may ask, for example, how the student knows or imagines the speaker has arrived at sea, offering many possible options. Ideally, the options should emerge from the students' remarks and at the same time help them connect one student's comments to another's, and to interconnect locations or the time frames (minutes, hours, days, years, etc.) in which students understand the events to have occurred or be occurring. Thus the single question *What is the situation?* reveals the narrative essence of a poem, as well as its time, setting, and conflict. Once participants have been drawn into the poem, and have enlarged the space of the poem so that their imaginations can move about freely within limits, establishing possibilities that they will be able to develop and refine later on, it may be time to shift to another, related aspect of the poem. The first area, narration in this instance, has by no means been exhausted; rather, it has been, for the purpose of the class, sufficiently enlarged.

To reach this point, the presentation and timing of the questions and options are as important as the questions and options themselves. Teaching poetry is a dynamic process. The teacher must not confirm or deny students' responses but rather acknowledge them, and with a question or oblique comment, lead students to review their reactions or relate them to ones they have already heard. An answer may be met with a question or counterstatement including, if appropriate, facts that contradict it. Or, if possible, the teacher may bring it face-to-face with a different or even contradictory possibility. Whenever possible another student, not the teacher, should lead the first student to reconsider his or her observations. By sustaining the interplay between responses and opinions, without favoring or disapproving of any, the teacher can encourage a multidimensional rather than linear discussion and understanding of a poem. This procedure can be used with every aspect of a poem. Of course, as the exploration of the poem proceeds, observations and discoveries made in one area will be carried over and related to discoveries in many other areas.

When the time seems ripe to leave the story line for another area such as point of view, the students bring along the understanding they gained from their discussion of the story line. Moreover, at any time they may briefly return to the story line for information concerning point of view.

No doubt it will seem difficult during the discussion of the tory line of "Western Wind" to avoid talking about the person to whom the events are occurring or at least to consider who may be involved in them. Some students usually refer to the speaker anonymously or use the third person singular masculine pronoun, *he*. To shift to the area of speaker identity, and again to force back the walls of the discussion, the teacher might simply ask, "How do you know this is a he or a she?" or "Who is this person?" Current critical theory bears out the practice, common especially to post-Romantic poets, of creating speakers distinct from the poets themselves. The question of identity is bountiful, and the teacher should be ready, at appropriate intervals, to introduce or recognize the possibilities of the narrator's sex, age, occupation, class, country of origin, and so on. The poem may not definitively answer the identity question. But considerable material may be found in the poem relating to the speaker. Given the situations students have discussed, would the speaker more likely be a woman or a man? Is it possible to tell? Does the narrative preclude a child or an elderly man or woman from being the speaker? Why or why not? Has historical information arisen in the discussion that can direct us to a likely occupation for the speaker? Is there a speaker, or is someone dreaming? Is the speaker human, or has the poet imagined a plant or animal conversing? These are all rich possibilities that can be accepted and followed, at least for a time. Eventually, a range of likely possibilities for the speaker's identity will develop that can be debated by the class. Then the possibilities may be discussed in conjunction with another of the poem's areas of expression, possibly the poem's structure or the speaker's language.

The brevity and simplicity of "Western Wind" may lead naturally to a discussion of the poem's form. The students may be asked whether the manner in which the speaker has arranged his or her thoughts and feelings is revealing in any way. The discussion of "plot" and speaker will have stimulated students' imaginations to offer suggestions concerning form that stem from what they know about the plot. They may be urged to consider how a person of a certain age or background in a given situation--lost at sea, for example--might respond to a crisis. How would the thoughts and feelings of such a person in a predicament differ from those of a younger man, of a woman, of an experienced seafarer, and so forth? Who would be more likely to remain calm, who to panic, who to despair?

Within such a framework, students will eventually discover two significant structural facets of "Western Wind." First, they will notice that the first two lines of the poem are in the form of a question. Second, they will find that the tone of address in the poem changes abruptly from the first two to the last two lines. The poem's abruptness of form mirrors the utterances of someone who is likely to shift moods suddenly. Of course, in the context of an unstable situation such as this poem's, this category could include many people. Yet this abrupt shift includes a reference (curse or plea) to a force above or beyond the speaker. Who would call the Western Wind "thou," and beseech it to moisten a barren place or state of mind, and then suddenly cry out in anger or loss of control for his or her love and the solace of his or her own bed? This challenging question also contains a time dimension. How much time, if any, has passed between the reaction of the first two lines and the cry of the second pair? Is there an interval? Has the speaker considered or remembered something new in the last two lines? Has something happened? Happily, these questions cannot be isolated from concerns of story and speaker. In fact, understanding form is a prerequisite to understanding the story; form is a manifestation of the speaker that leads the student more fully to the poem's center.

The speaker's words themselves now demand to be heard. They can no longer be disentangled from narrative, voice, or form. Students will know him, her, or it not only by what is said but by the words used to say it. What is distinctive about the speaker's language? What will his or her words add to our understanding of the story, situation, and dynamic of the poem? Often, they help us determine which of the ways we have been looking at the poem best fit the poem itself. The speaker's language--its sentences, words, sounds, and even pauses--reveal much of the essence of the speaker's plight, personality, and thought process. If the words *small rain*, for example, reveal an especially delicate sensibility, this will affect our sense of how the speaker reacts to his or her situation, and in fact of the speaker's identity. If the awkward syntax--the absence of expected transition *so that*--seems to indicate a psyche under pressure, then it will help the reader decide among the choices about the speaker's situation that would be considered early in a class session. How does the speaker intend the word *Christ*? Does the exclamation point at the close of the poem indicate shock, anger, dismay, or some other feeling? What precisely does the alliteration in the first line (*Western wind when wilt* . . .) reveal about the speaker's state of mind? In any poem, but certainly in a poem of 26 words, the language of the main speaker reveals the course of the poem, which, through observations of narration, speaker, and form, students have been following. Solidly on course, we can stay with the flow as it takes us to the meanings of the poem--the themes.

The students will now be ready and eager for a full discussion of the poem's meaning. Other aspects of poetic expression, such as irony, paradox, myth, and symbol, may be discussed before or during a discussion of theme. But for the most part the concerns from which ideas are formed about a poem's theme have already been explored. No doubt students have also touched on the area of theme and perhaps hazarded guesses about it. At this point, however, the first formal discussion of theme should begin.

While all the aspects of a poem previously discussed are background for and essential to discussing theme, students do not ordinarily make the jump to theme smoothly. To overcome this reaction, the facilitator can ask several questions. Why are this situation and this speaker important to us? Why do we care about what is going on here? These two questions are other ways of asking what is universal in this situation. Another approach, more closely linked to the class's previous discussion, is to ask what we have discovered about the situation with which we began. What do all the poetic components have in common? What is the speaker feeling about the situation? If either of the two kinds of questions elicits the response that desire or frustration, or some kindred feeling, dominates the poem, then the discussion of theme has begun. Encourage the students to elaborate on their responses; ask them to specify the patterns and details of this frustration and desire. Ask them to consider what the speaker desires. If it is fertility that the speaker is after, what kind of fertility is it? What are its manifestations? If reactions to absence and longing are involved, then what prevents the speaker from obtaining what is missing? Draw out such responses, even when they won't bring definitive answers. Of course, students should and will weave these forays into theme with the understanding they have accumulated from the discussion of narration, speaker, form, and language.

The class discussion should culminate in a one-sentence, capsule statement of the theme--the universal meaning of the poem. Students may state several such sentences, then work together to capture the universality for which they have striven. They may work as a group toward producing a statement that reflects a compromise among conflicting ideas and includes the essential viewpoints. The result should be a theme statement or statements, not the final meaning of the poem for all time but the class's tentative account of the major universal thrust of the poem. For "Western Wind," one possible statement might read as follows: "Expression of the deepest despair, the strongest rage, or the most fervent pleas may sometimes be all one can do in a difficult situation." Not all students or all facilitators will be completely happy with this or any other statement of the poem's theme. For example, some may say, rightly, that this statement does not reflect the disruption of the normal life cycle emphasized in the poem. However, satisfaction usually comes from the process itself of having explored and come to know a poem in some depth.

Principles for Teaching Poetry in the ESL Setting

This overview of teaching "Western Wind" contains the outlines of a general approach to poetry. The following guidelines can be drawn.

First, identify the approaches that are best suited to the poem at hand. Although most approaches prove useful for any poem, each poem responds better to one or another particular approach. In preparing your lesson, look over the poem carefully, noting its most significant features. For example, if, as in "Western Wind," the situation portrayed from the start is a need or a request for the wind to blow and the rain to rain, you may pursue this with questions. A search for the possible reasons for the request is an obvious approach. Asking who may be making the request follows logically. The location of the speaker also seems to require investigation. Here the experiential (a poem rooted in a person, place, and time) approach is indicated. Of course, in this approach, these questions inevitably lead to others--order, language, and so on. If a poem begins with a comparison, as does Shakespeare's sonnet Number 130 (*My mistress's eyes are nothing like the sun*), comparing his mistress's body to objects of beauty, then the sequence and unity of the comparisons may determine the approach: *eyes*, *lips*, and so on. Thus an approach corresponds to the directions the reader may take in enjoying and understanding a poem based on the clearest signals it emits--narrative, structural, experiential, or other.

Second, begin your presentation with an oral reading of the poem. Poetry has its origins in singing, and music in general is basic to it; it is an auditory experience. Ideally, the students themselves should read the poem. If possible, before the reading, review the pronunciation of words, the rhythms, the fact that line endings don't require stops, and other basics. Have them practice reading at home. Then ask some students to read the entire poem or individual students to read parts (lines or stanzas) of the poem. There is no harm in reading the poem more than once. It helps the students to feel comfortable with the poem, and may stimulate them to observe and question the differing tones of the readings. You yourself may also read the poem aloud once. The first five minutes of a poetry lesson are often pivotal. Reading the poem aloud can ensure its success. When the lesson is finished, have students, with their new understanding of the poem, reread it aloud.

Third, begin questioning with the story or narrative base of the poem. Since all poems contain some narrative element, this is always a good place to scan for a possible start. Identifying a plot, or sequence of events, often makes it easier to grasp the outlines of a poem. Even poems with no overt narrative often assume a background of events. In addition, students feel freer to explore the poem once they have absorbed the surface meaning.

Fourth, encourage students to make connections among various aspects of the poem, rather than seeking out definitive answers.

Keep afloat a range of controlled possibilities about the poem. At each stage of the process of discovering a poem, participants are prone to leap to conclusions or reach for answers they think they have found. To avoid these premature interpretations, the facilitator should strive to prolong pluralistic visions of a poem. Suggest and reinforce relationships between questions already asked and those presently being asked, between points already made and those presently on the table. Encourage the students to fully express the possibilities that come to mind after examining various parts of a poem. The chief advantage of this approach is that it keeps students alert to the subtle relationships among the poem's parts--noticing how, for example, understanding of a speaker's voice may be a reaction to a certain situation. In short, the discussion should be dynamic, moving toward a grasp of the poem rather than toward a mechanically preordained interpretation. Tell students that finding connections between interlocking parts of the whole poem, and not a bland statement of the poet's entire meaning, is the goal. Release the students from the tyranny of seeking answers; let the discovery of the poem's possibilities and unity emerge.

Fifth, conceive of the poem from various dimensions: visual, auditory, sensory, structural, and so forth. It is a truism that nothing can be seen completely from one angle alone. Poetry is no exception. If envisioned from multiple points of view, it will blossom in various hues. Allow yourself and your students the luxury of many lenses and many viewing locations. If a discussion bogs down in one area, such as structural, turn students' attention to the senses the poem speaks to. In short, a multiplicity of viewpoints enhances the study of any poem.

Sixth, provide for the understanding but not the meanings of unfamiliar vocabulary, allusions, and background. As the class discussion of a poem proceeds, students may occasionally feel blocked when they encounter an unfamiliar word or cultural allusion. At times, a historical, social, or religious reference is the basis of a poem or a part of it. If poems have been well-selected and prepared for nonnative readers, this should occur infrequently. When it does come up, however, handle the obstacle as part of the process of reaching more deeply into the poem. Determine whether the information is really needed at the time it first comes up. Is it essential to their grasp and enjoyment of the poem? If not, encourage the students to move on and return to it later when additional information or understanding may clear it up. Otherwise, encourage alternate methods for students to grapple with the crucial reference. If the words or allusions are essential, do not provide the meanings yourself. Assign each student, early on, at least as a first try, one word or allusion to report on to the class. Handled this way, the task does not become too arduous for any one person. Even if the student cannot come up with the meaning or the full sense of the allusion, he or she will provide a beginning in the process of understanding the reference. Other students or the facilitator, who may know the culture better, may use their knowledge to fill in any missing gaps. The unfamiliar in the poem becomes, then, not a dreary obstacle but another step in the excitement of reaching more deeply into the poem.

Seventh, don't lose sight of the poem's uniqueness and wholeness. Each poem creates its own world and, if the poem is effective, each part of its world is consistent with every other part. The particular world never existed before and may never exist again. It is both coherent and ephemeral. Yet, as we have seen, its coherence is comprehensible. It yields the same kind of answers to the same questions people ask of their daily lives: Why do we like one person and dislike another? How can we overcome our fear of the unknown future? Why am I bored with my job?

How to Teach a Poem: A Model

> There was never any more inception than there is now,
> Nor any more youth or age than there is now,
> And will never be any more perfection than there is now.
>
> Walt Whitman, "Song of Myself" III

You are never readier, the American poet Walt Whitman (1819-1892) tells us in these words, than you are now. You may know more, or feel more confident at a later date, but at this moment you are as prepared as you will ever be to enter and understand a poem. Poetry accepts you at your current level of readiness--no matter what it is. This is most certainly true of "Those Winter Sundays," written by the black American poet Robert Hayden (1913-1980).

Those Winter Sundays

Sundays too my father got up early
and put his clothes on in the blueblack cold,

Note. From *Angle of Ascent: New and Selected Poems* by R. Hayden, 1975, New York: Liveright. Copyright 1975 by Liveright. Reprinted by permission.

>   then with cracked hands that ached
>   from labor in the weekday weather made
>   banked fires blaze. No one ever thanked him.
>
>   I'd wake and hear the cold splintering, breaking.
>   When the rooms were warm, he'd call,
>   and slowly I would rise and dress,
>   fearing the chronic angers of that house,
>
>   Speaking indifferently to him
>   who had driven out the cold
>   and polished my good shoes as well.
>   What did I know, what did I know
>   of love's austere and lonely offices?

The poem asks you in. You seem to enter into the middle of a conversation with someone you know only slightly. So conversational is the poem's beginning that it is deceptive. The speaker seems to want to talk about some shopping he or she did, a good bargain found, or his or her day at work. The first few words of a poem, always significant, seem rather casual here. The words are so basic, so mundane, so unnoticeable: a day of the week, a person, a possessive adjective defining the relationship. Yet the ordinarily simple adverb *too* carries with it a pull, for it suggests that you and the speaker have been speaking about his or her father's action, in a part of the conversation that precedes the start of the poem. Thus it seems you are not entering a poem but continuing your involvement in an ongoing situation.

What kind of situation is it? The title suggests the subject is not just one day, one Sunday, but many Sundays, perhaps years of Sundays. Again, the title hints at earlier conversations and shared previous knowledge of the days being referred to: Those Sundays were winter Sundays. The situation is not a current one, since *those* suggests a past time, but in this poem you are involved in a current discussion about them. The title, then, adds useful information, including (a) that you, the listener, have previously discussed these times--that is, the subject is not totally new to you; (b) that those days are past; (c) that they were special, nonroutine days--Sundays, days of rest or quiet thought; and (d) that they were in the Northern Hemisphere, cold days with less light than in other warmer seasons. The first four words have established a familiar, even congenial tone, banishing any abruptness. The speaker and you, the listener, have been conversing comfortably and continue to do so.

What other information does the speaker choose to tell? The speaker focuses not directly on his or her own life but on the effects of the father's actions. Although the father never speaks, he dominates the first stanza. We learn that he got up early on cold Sundays, just as he did on weekdays, that he was probably an outdoor or factory worker, as indicated by his aching hands cracking from his work; that, nevertheless, he started the morning fire to warm up the icy house. In the second and third stanzas we are told that after the fire was burning strongly, he would call his child. The child would find that the father had also shined his child's special (*good*) shoes. As one student, Kolb (1983), has observed:

> Clearly, the father is not a lazy man, nor one who felt the world owed him a living. After working all week, his hands aching and cracked from the hard work and cold winter weather, this man could have chosen to stay in bed on Sunday mornings. . . . Instead we see this man rise quite early in the morning, get dressed in the bitter cold, warm the house with a blazing fire, and polish his child's shoes. He didn't insist his child should get up with him. His attitude is a caring and unselfish one, as we see him allowing his child to sleep while he attends to taking the chill out of the cold house. We can see how considerate this man is in that he doesn't wake his child until the house is sufficiently warmed. We don't hear him complaining or expressing bitterness about his life situation, so he seems to be an accepting rather than an angry type of individual. He knows apparently how to love unconditionally, even when his child shows no appreciation and speaks indifferently to him. (p.1)

This is what we know or can infer from the narrator's words.

The remaining information the speaker provides concerns his or her own responses or lack of responses to the father. "No one," including presumably this child, "ever thanked him." When called on those cold Sundays, the child would respond slowly, reluctant to enter the turmoil and anger of the house. The child says he or she spoke to the father without feeling. This, then, is what the speaker recalls and tells of those years. Of course, in looking back, the speaker may not understand all that has occurred since then, or not be able or wish to recall or reveal all the details of that period.

With what words, images, details, sounds, sentences, rhymes, and rhythm the speaker recounts his or her experience is as important as what he or she reveals. Rereading the poem with the notion of winter in mind, notice that the opposition of two categories of words the speaker uses stands out: warm and cold. The father dresses in the *blueblack cold*, and the child's words to him are *indifferently frigid*. They have neither color nor heat. Love is *austere and lonely*, words that evoke coolness. On the other hand, the father makes *banked fires blaze* hotly. The cold, like wood, splinters and breaks under the heat's intensity. Hottest of all are the *chronic angers* the child so fears. Anger may arise from cold motives or reactions, but is inherently hot-blooded. Throughout the poem, these two temperature extremes contend with each other.

The very sounds of the words are steamy with heat or frosted over with an icy glaze. The *k* sounds in *blueblack, cracked, thanked, cold, clothes, chronic,* and *call* stir us to cold realization of the tension in the house. Ice resides in the *l*s and *o*s of *slowly, know,* and even *love*. But flames issue from the *b*s of *blaze, breaking,* and *labors,* and the *g*s and *n*s of *chronic, angers,* and the obviously hot sound of *fires*.

The selection of hard, mechanical actions the speaker has presented is reinforced with monosyllabic verbs: *put, ached, made, thanked, wake, hear, call, rise, dress,* and *know*. This series of single-syllable words conveys a world with sharp edges only and no rounded corners. These verbs make up more than ten percent of the poem's 97 words. The sentences reinforce the harshness and trepidation the narrator experienced in the home environment. A long (32-word) sentence description of the father's action, leading the reader to believe more description will follow, is interrupted abruptly by the five-word sentence, *No one ever thanked him*. Another brief sentence follows. Then another long (38-word), sweeping sentence appears. Finally, a sharp question, repeated, ends the poem. *What did I know? What did I know . . . .* The alternation of long sentences with short but significant interruptions mirrors the speaker's unstable life, as it is recalled for us. The speaker has no opportunity, and gives his listeners none, once they are involved in the poem, to steady themselves, to find solid emotional ground.

The rhyme, likewise, is only partial--half-rhyme or internal rhyme, and no full end-of-line rhymes. *Dress* echoes sounds of but does not rhyme with *offices*. *Breaking* and *ached* have the same relationship. Only *banked* and *thanked* fully rhyme. Two end words are simply repeated: *him* and *cold*. There is no smooth, tranquil rounding off of the lines, only sharp reminders of the bind in which parent and child find themselves.

What kind of person would frame such an account? Who is speaking? What can we conclude about the speaker from the details presented and the words, sound, and rhythms chosen to explain them? The speaker's geographical location, other than in a cold climate, does not seem to affect the events. His or her occupation or even sex does not much matter, though the speaker's working-class origins are likely. Age may be of importance, to be discussed shortly, because of the passage of time in the poem. The speaker's character has the greatest effect. He or she is clearly the father's child: Like the father, the child is sensitive and observant, with a good eye for detail. The speaker vividly remembers exactly what the father did for him or her, and phrases the actions in crisp, precise language. The speaker is also an inherently honest person, presenting an account that includes not only the father's virtues but also the narrator's own shortcomings. Sentimentality does not take over in this poem; it is countered by specific details of the narrator's own behavior.

The narrator's most important traits, also akin to the father's, are courage and the ability to change and grow. After all, the speaker takes a hard look at a painful experience of long ago and reevaluates it from a new position. Both processes--the look back and the reevaluation--must be difficult. Both require the courage and the willingness to review and revise perhaps long-held and comfortable concepts of oneself. The sounds of the poem, the uneven syntax, and the repetition at the end all suggest that the speaker is upset. Yet, despite some flinching, the speaker summons up the experiences, probing and reconsidering them, persisting to the end. The speaker's integrity and bravery are unquestionable.

Considering how much time has elapsed since the events of the poem, those winter Sundays, these characteristics are even more telling. The speaker presumably has not lived in the poem's location for years, but has willingly transported himself or herself emotionally back to the place and time. The painfulness of the journey is suggested by the off-balance structure of the poem itself. Through 12 of the poem's 14 lines, the speaker recalls all of the father's acts. Only in the final two lines does the speaker finally hone in on and acknowledge the pain of recall. Stirring these old ashes has taken the speaker over a considerable poetic journey as well. The poem should progress, and has done so, but only to arrive at the dead end of ineradicable pain. It takes 12 lines of detailed recall for the speaker to admit the pain. The space of years and the distance in miles, rather than extinguishing the excruciatingly painful realization, have merely brought it to a head.

The theme of the poem begins to emerge here. As time has passed, and the speaker has moved away from childhood, he or she, the son or daughter of a now deceased or somehow unavailable father, has come to appreciate the quality of the *austere and lonely offices* the father carried out for the child. The speaker now recognizes how the father continued to do so despite his family's indifference, and now clearly comprehends this parent's chief virtue: the ability to love unconditionally. Yet, despite the time, effort, and anguish involved in the child's realization, it is nevertheless, in one sense, too late to make any difference. The speaker may still use the newfound understanding for his or her own benefit, but it is too late to communicate it to the father for a reason the poem does not provide. But it is clearly too late for the child to communicate his or her understanding, appreciation, and love to the father. The theme states that people may grow, learn, and even snatch for a moment a vision of what it means to love. Still, we are prevented from acting on or sharing what we have learned. It takes time--often a long time--the poet stresses, to learn to love, and sometimes, even after all this time, it is too late to put our learning to use with and for others. The child has definitely learned something about love from the father and from experience, as the use of the past tense in *What did I know?* and the knowledge now of those *austere and lonely offices* suggests, but he or she is, ironically, prevented from passing along that knowledge or love to the person perhaps most important in the speaker's life--the father.

To arrive at such a statement of theme, which is, of course, only one way among many of seeing the poem, a worksheet such a the following may serve as a guide both to you and to your students. A worksheet is only an application of the questioning technique explained earlier. The questions for any poem concern story, speaker, form, language, rhyme, rhythm, character, and theme. They may be considered in any order, and the worksheet may be introduced either for homework before beginning the class discussion or at the beginning of the class itself.

Worksheet for "Those Winter Sundays"

I. Narrative Base

1. Is there a story or plot in the poem, either stated or unstated? That is, what, if anything, "happens" in the poem?

2. Does the speaker suggest a conflict or struggle between two or more antagonistic forces? If so, try to state the nature of the struggle.

3. What is the scene or location of the poem? Is there a specific setting? Is it real or imagined? Fantasize about where this might have taken place or might now take place.

4. Does the title help you to understand the situation of the poem?

II. Speaker

1. Does the speaker adhere to a single point of view? Observe the pronouns and any change in them. Is this a first-person poem? Is the speaker alone?

2. Why has the speaker chosen to remember a time and place so distant?

3. Draw a mental picture of the speaker's physical presence in your imagination. How do you see him or her? Explain your vision.

III. Form or Structure

1. Is the time passage of the poem given? If not, how much time do you think has passed? Why?

2. Are there noticeable divisions in the poem? Where do they occur? For example, why does the poem have three stanzas? Is the number 14, the number of lines in the poem, important?

3. Why does the poem end with a question?

IV. Language, Rhyme, and Rhythm

1. Make a list of five "warm" words in the poem and five "cold" words. What gives each group it special quality?

2. What are the predominant sounds in the poem? What do they suggest about the speaker's state of mind?

V. Character

Suppose that the father was present to answer his child. What would he say? Write a brief paragraph (50 words) giving his response.

VI. Theme

1. What does the title suggest about the theme of the poem?

2. Is the speaker presenting an objective point of view from the position of remembering years later?

Criteria for Choosing Poems

The preceding discussion of "Western Wind" and "Those Winter Sundays" should provide a clear idea of the kinds of poems that are suitable for use with ESL students. Poems found in poetry anthologies and in volumes by individual poets should meet most if not all of the following conditions, although these conditions are by no means exhaustive. You may incorporate other measures to help make poetry both an appropriate and a delightful experience for your students.

First, length is not a primary criterion of teachability. A brief poem may compress so much material in a short space that it is quite difficult. However, a class session, preceded by a brief preparatory homework assignment, should be sufficient for students to master the essence of most poems chosen. For longer poems, students should be able to grasp at least a third of the poem in no more than a single class session. If students must spend too long an interval between when they first enter the poem and when they reach far enough into its depths to understand it, they may feel the rewards are too few over too long a stretch of time. Limited-English-proficient students may be reluctant to continue.

Second, the subject matter of the poem selected should present a universal and timeless theme. No one poem, of course, can or needs to include the experience of all races, ages, class backgrounds, nationalities, sexual identities, and sexual preferences. Yet a poem can and should mean something to a great number of people in all these categories. No one can predict which poem will do so or can state exactly how to present a poem so that it will. Yet poems that are immersed in specific locales, times, and situations often very effectively communicate universal themes.

A poem such as Dudley Randall's (1981) "Ballad of Birmingham," which tells of the death of a child killed in the bombing of a black church in Mississippi in the 1960s, could hardly be of more regional subject matter. Yet Randall brings out the reader's universal feelings at the needless death of a child. So it may be a paradox, but certainly not a conflict, that the local and timely often encompass the universal and timeless. In a truly universal and timeless poem, each reader, no matter where or when he or she is living, should to some degree be able to relate to the poem, even without fully comprehending, liking, or agreeing with the poet's views. No easy labels identify poems with universal themes, but in selecting poetry for class presentation, the teacher should always probe the poem to discover universality that may not show up with a quick look at the apparent subject matter, setting, or other apparatus. Probe the poem to discover conflicts in which all people may feel involved and resolutions in which most may rejoice.

Third, the poem should focus on feelings. Many poems take on the very hefty subject of history, of an idea, of a mythological tale. Such materials often result in very beautiful and significant poems. But for the nonnative reader of English, a poem that takes an emotion as its main subject may be both more comfortable and more pleasurable. Look for poems that bring into play the reader's capacity to empathize and sympathize, to feel the full range of universal human emotions.

Fourth, find poems that challenge the students. Charlesworth (1978) provides some evidence that in the long run students prefer and respond more intelligently and sensitively to challenging, even complex poetry than they do to poems simple enough for them to grasp quickly and effortlessly. A review of James Emmanuel's *A Poet's Mind* (Sage, 1983) raises some of these considerations. This point is also reflected in the list of anthologies for study on page 89. Ferret out the stimulating, difficult poems. Even poetry with complex syntax, obscure allusions, and unfamiliar words can become accessible.

Although it may seem desirable to identify a firm level of poetry appropriate for ESL students, it is more useful, and more honest, for the individual teacher to try to describe the qualities of poetry that would best match specific students' levels. An innovative facilitator can surmount apparent obstacles and even turn them into a stimulus for students to learn more. In the preceding discussion of two poems, ways to do so have already been described, and in the next chapter on model classroom activities with poetry, several more will be described. For now, recall that even with a complex poem, you need not stress the obstacles. The difficult-to-reach riches of a challenging poem can be a catalyst for students to explore further and discover more.

The following checkpoints may help a teacher who is unsure about matching the level of the poems chosen to the student:

1. After reading the poem once, can you see the outlines of a situation (speaker, time, and place) in the poem?

2. Do you notice at least five lines anywhere in the poem that you understand well enough on the literal level to paraphrase? Would the five lines help you to understand other lines you do not understand at first?

3. Would you find it possible to ask useful questions about the content of the poem? For example, does the poem take place in the present? Is the poem moving in a certain clear direction?

You will probably not respond positively to all the checkpoints, but if even one or two are useful to you, the poem's accessibility ratio, the extent to which it allows readers to enter and understand, is sufficient for you to try the poem with your students.

These checkpoints are not unalterable rules. Apply them flexibly and freely, and with balance. If the three criteria work well enough for you then the weight of the evidence suggests that the poem--even a relatively difficult poem--is appropriate for your students.

Classroom Activities During and After Discussion of a Poem

No poetry lesson is complete without activities that transform the poem from an object of discussion into a living force as alive and as much a part of our world as water, plants, animals, and people. The variety of such activities is surely infinite. So is their potential for getting students excited about poetry. Because there are so many possible activities, only a few are described here in detail, while others will be touched on briefly so that the interested facilitator or student may look into them individually.

One basic poetry activity calls on students' aural/oral interests and abilities. Reading poems aloud, listening to good recordings of poems, such as those on the Cademon label, or, if possible, arranging for readings by the poets themselves, are all ways to enhance the experience of poetry. The student should repeat the poem after hearing it, imitating certain sounds in the poem. Feeling your own lips pronounce the sounds gives you a special sense of the poet's composing process. Such repetition of sounds should accompany an analysis of selected important sounds in the poem, as was demonstrated for "Those Winter Sundays."

Beyond the oral/aural experience of the poem itself, role plays are another effective oral experience. Ask the students, in pairs perhaps, to perform role plays of the speaker, elaborating on the speaker's words and extending the speaker's feelings to contexts other than the immediate contexts of the poem. After an extended period, students will get a sense of the speaker's person that is not possible through reading alone. A poem, being only a situation or a slice of the speaker's life, can be enriched by a student's extending the situation to other slices. The Russian novelist Turgenev was said to have followed the living sources for his characters around for months and to have compiled long biographies of them simply to extract a few details about them for a paragraph or two in a novel. In this manner, he sought to attain verisimilitude. Here the process is reversed, extrapolating from the poet's selection to role-play a speaker's entire life.

Activities supporting the class's work in poetry may also draw on students' artistic skills and interests. To discover how students visualize a poem, nothing can be more efficient and exciting than to have them make a rough sketch of how they see the poem's setting. Students' inclusion or exclusion of telling details, the placement of objects, and the relative proportion of details all reveal how they imagine the poet's words. With "Those Winter Sundays," for example, the students could roughly sketch the house. For those who do not or will not draw, a verbal drawing also tells a great deal about how they see the poem. A sketch is a student's reconstruction of something seen only by the poet; it appears in pictorial form for the first time at the student's hands. It is at once cathartic for the student and informative to the facilitator about the student's insight into the poem.

Putting previously learned linguistic skills to use in activities, including written activities, is enjoyable for limited-English-proficient students. An easy and appealing activity has students fill in missing letters of words in a certain grammatical or semantic category. For example, they may be asked to write adjectives from "Those Winter Sundays" that describe cold and heat or their effects. Students then might complete *c__ck__d (cracked), br__ki__ (breaking), ac__d (ached), ba__ke__ (banked), spl__nt__i__g (splintering)* (McConochie, 1982). A cloze exercise is a variation of the same idea. Students are asked to supply a word that might fit in the blank and then compare the choices they make with the poet's actual choices, as follows (McConochie, 1982):

> Western Wind, when _____ _____ blow
> The _____ rain down can rain?
> Christ! if my _____ were in my _____
> And I in my _____ again!

Sentence decombining provides still another opportunity for students to enter into the arrangement and rearrangement of a poem in order to better understand it. The process consists of dividing compound, complex, and compound-complex sentences into simple sentences. Students can then put them in the order in which they would occur in nonpoetic usage and observe, as McConochie (1982) points out, the differences from the poetic arrangement.

Another activity that can help students understand the form of a poem is the strip story (Gibson, 1975). Students are given three-by-five cards that each contain a single line of the poem. As a group, they are then asked to put the poem back together again. In so doing, they can discover the poet's organizational strategy as well as transitions. For a description of other such activities, for example "cultural translation" (Pincas, 1963), see McConochie's (1982) excellent explanation and application of these activities to particular poems and Povey's (1979) critique of Pincas' presentation.

Finally, students should be encouraged to write their own poetry, as Preston (1982) and Maher (1981) demonstrate. Students may enjoy writing "found" poems, poems based on materials that ordinarily appear in the environment, such as graffiti, advertisements, announcements, and other everyday speech. They may also enjoy creating concrete poetry (Brod, 1983), or poetry that is shaped rather than written and often depends on visual perception to produce its effects. These are especially good warm-up exercises at the start of a poetry class. On a more serious note, refugees, as Kuntz (1986) explains, may find relief for their feelings by writing poetry based on their experiences.

Other activities may draw on aspects of the activities just discussed, perhaps noting the logical structure of a given poem and comparing it to other possible logical schemes. Through a new combination, a new activity is created. For example, noting the syllogistic form of certain poems and having students state the components of this structure, as with the Countee Cullen poem, "Incident," is a handy entrance to a poem. The poet describes a situation, a given; relates an occurrence that altered it; and draws the conclusion. Is it a logical conclusion? By formulating a syllogistic pattern, the students rapidly discover the poem's emotional substratum. A listing of all the contrasts in a given poem, cold and heat, light and dark, and so forth, also often clarifies a work. Tracing the pronouns and their shifts within a poem may point up how the speaker's attention or focus has shifted or has not shifted. In Blake's "A Poison Tree," the speaker is obsessed with killing his neighbor, and uses a first person form no fewer than 15 times in 16 lines.

Ultimately, however, straightforward discussion of a poem should be neither forgotten nor abandoned. Asking students to bring their own experience into play with questions concerning a poem is a tried, venerable, and still effective way to involve students in poetry. Ask students to express their views of the speaker's or the poet's feelings. Do they agree with them? The limits on the kinds of questions that can be posed concerning a poem are no narrower or wider than the facilitator's imagination and the students' ability and willingness to suspend disbelief and speculate on the possible meanings of a line, a stanza, or an entire poem. There is nothing passé or boring about raising questions that stimulate students to look more sensitively at poetry. Good questions about poetry and good poetry itself are available in all places and all times. As Keats writes in "On the Grasshopper and Cricket" (1959, p. 19):

> The poetry of earth is never dead:
>   When all the birds are faint with the hot sun,
>   And hide in cooling trees, a voice will run
> From hedge to hedge about the new-mown mead;
> That is the Grasshopper's--he takes the lead
>   In summer luxury,--he has never done
>   With his delights; for when tired out with fun
> He rests at ease beneath some pleasant weed.
> The poetry of earth is ceasing never:
>   On a lone winter evening, when the frost
>   Has wrought a silence, from the stove there shrills
> The Cricket's song, in warmth increasing ever,
>   And seems to one in drowsiness half lost,
>   The Grasshopper's among some grassy hills.

4

Teaching Short Stories in the ESL Classroom

Short fiction, both spoken and written, permeates life. Nevertheless, people's image of short fiction may be difficult to put into words. Most publishers of short story books for ESL students have not felt the necessity to do so. Those who do attempt to define the term *short fiction*, as does Mullen (1984), do so only briefly and with reference not to linguistic concerns but to the short story in literary tradition. But a good definition is clearly needed.

For one thing, most people do not have as strong a grasp or as good a memory of the tradition as specialists may. Current-Garcia and Patrick (1961) present many of the important documents of the short story tradition, both by critics and by the writers themselves, and a fine collection of stories from many countries to discuss and enjoy. Second, and from the ESL point of view, it is important if not to redefine short fiction, at least to look at it in the context of ESL research in related areas--spoken narratives, use of time in actual conversation, and similar matters.

Few, if any, ESL works define short fiction. In studies and descriptions of narration, it is often unclear whether oral or written narratives are being discussed. White (1977), after stating that narration essentially recounts what has already occurred, identifies its formal features as including chronological sequence, markers to indicate it, and the use of the past tense. This definition is informative precisely because it is so limited. It reveals instantly its inappropriateness for a study of the short story in which the past is one--but only one--of the focal points and tenses used. Clearly, many differences exist between narratives, as often discussed in linguistic literature, and short fiction--both spoken, as in early oral traditions, and written.

Abercrombie (1963) draws a few important distinctions between written prose and spoken language. He points out that in the early 1960s linguistics was paying considerable attention to spoken prose rather than other forms of spoken language. He enumerates several specific differences between spoken prose and genuine conversation. He even relates spoken prose, the naturalistic dialogue of literature, to everyday conversation and states that even in fiction no one speaks as people actually do in conversation. Abercrombie's points may be disputed, but he contributes the idea of comparing what linguists know and are learning about conversational narratives with the narrative base of short fiction. Fiction, as a rendering of people's dreams, actions, and words, may indeed have points of contact with conversational language. Wolfson (1979) and DiPietro (1983) offer ways to relate the characteristics of spoken prose as Wolfson, for example, describes them, to similar fictionalized narratives. This kind of comparison will go a long way toward a description of the essence of short fiction, one that ESL students and teachers can use.

A focus on narratives widens the base for a definition of short fiction. A working definition appropriate for ESL may begin with the narrative. Until such a definition is developed, however, an inductive approach may be necessary. By simply observing and enjoying the stories at hand, teachers and students may build an extended definition of the short story appropriate to their needs.

A Rationale for the Use of Fiction in ESL

Definitions are often elusive. So, too, very often, are rationales. The difficulty of promoting the value of a good short story is unquestionable. Once again, the inductive method is a useful preliminary step in explaining why short fiction deserves to be part of the ESL curriculum.

A good story is a joy. Short fiction helps impart both pleasure and knowledge to nonnative students. Neither must be postponed or sacrificed. Most stories, whether they deal with serious or comic matters, are simply fun to read and discuss. As Potter (1983) aptly argues, teachers often overlook the fact that students would simply like to enjoy reading fiction. She suggests that such pleasure comes not only from reading works of permanent literary merit but also from light fiction reading. The light fiction, she says, should visually resemble books for native speakers, have no accompanying study materials, and be short and low-priced. Reading short fiction can and should be pure hedonism.

No conflict exists between enjoying and learning through the short story. Reading short fiction undoubtedly improves students' language skills, in ways that are discussed here. McKay (1982) states that contemporary literary anthologies are based on the assumption that the study of literature helps improve students' language abilities and broaden their linguistic exposure. It can probably do so more effectively than the many ESL texts containing dialogues and role plays with scanty plot lines. These, as Widdowson (1982) has noted, relate only to a created context and are "dissimulations," not simulations (p. 207). Such pseudoliterary texts, as Widdowson refers to them, probably do not improve communication skills more efficiently than literature.

The same deficiency exists in many texts concerned with the teaching of cultural values. Unabridged and unmangled short stories present full cultural contexts. But because ESL readers often do not, "texts are needed which do, in fact, present the flow of normal conversation and which, when they form the basis for a freshman composition course for ESL students, can also provide an introduction to certain aspects of American culture" (Lezberg & Hilferty, 1978, p. 50). Literature, because one of its main goals is to reveal culture through character and story, succeeds more frequently than many other reading genres, such as exposition. Because much expository prose in ESL readers has journalistic origins, in seeking only to inform, it does not communicate the more subtle nuances of the society about which it reports. McKay (1980), reviewing Rosenblatt (1978), accurately distinguishes the expository from the fictional mode:

> Schools have traditionally given major emphasis to efferent reading and have thus tended to use a similar approach to aesthetic reading. Texts are used to develop language skills, both syntactic and lexical, and comprehen- sion is judged through paraphrase or restatement. . . . Students may conclude that all texts necessitate the same reader stance, and that ultimately the aim of all reading is to obtain information, to solve problems, to carry some- thing away. This minimizes the value of the very personal experience an individual reader can have with a literary text. (pp. 380-381)

Fiction writers have an obligation to entertain as well as to inform. Their stories are expected to hold the interest of readers over a certain period of time. For this reason, they must draw on and make use of a large and innovative storehouse of writing strategies. Deft handling of symbolic language and metaphor, insight into character, and varied and appropriate style are among the strategies that must be used in short fiction. The display of such strategies in the service of narrative for ESL student-witnesses gives fiction an important place in the ESL curriculum. In no other linguistic genre can nonnative students discover so much writing and language skill at work.

Short fiction is also a supreme resource for observing not only languge but life itself. In short fiction, characters act out all the real and symbolic acts people carry out in daily lives, and do so in a variety of registers and tones. Witness the following stories and their basic story lines: In William Carlos Williams' (1975) "The Use of Force," a doctor visits the home of a sick child whose parents strive to protect the child from the unfamiliar doctor. In Hemingway's "Ten Indians," a child is born, and the husband witnessing the painful birth commits suicide. In Ring Lardner's (1981) "Haircut," we overhear the gossip of a local barber shop. In "Only the Dead Know Brooklyn" (1962), Thomas Wolfe's story, an out-of-town subway rider's questions about directions to a native New York City rider lead the latter to reply that it is impossible for anyone to know Brooklyn, even those who live there all their lives. The world of short fiction both mirrors and illuminates human lives.

In addition to their inherent power, stories elicit students' natural desires to express their feelings through fiction. This opportunity is nothing new in literature, dating at least as far back as ancient Greek theater. Given that nonnative students' nonverbal language often indicates extreme frustration with their new language and suppressed anger, the instructor must help the student discover a route to catharsis. Fiction is such a route. Nonnative students want and need to tell stories. They want to share experiences and feelings. Doing so gives them an opportunity to alleviate the loneliness of being human beings, "islands of consciousness," in Branden's (1980) phrase. It allows them to listen and be distracted by the tales as well as to tell teachers and each other about their countries. Students can comfortably express feelings in English about themselves through the mask of a character. For someone whose English-language skills are developing, it is a safe experiment and a healthy outlet.

Some evidence exists that narratives are among the most comprehensible of messages. If so, they meet current views that a comprehensible message reinforces learning languages by keeping students' anxiety levels down and self-esteem high. In addition, as Wolf (1984) observes, "In narratives, speakers depend on types of linguistic skill which are barely tapped in single sentences. Therefore, until we study the language of narrators, we are bound to have a partial, and poorer, view of children's linguistic skills" (p. 845). According to Wolf, then, narratives facilitate the nonnative child's task of learning a second language. Perhaps children's ability to recognize coherence, setting, and other narrative elements as building from sentence to sentence in a narrative is something that holds true also for adult audiences. If so, this aspect is yet another reason for including short fiction in the ESL curriculum.

Finally, the inclusion of short fiction in the ESL curriculum offers three additional benefits. First, by definition, it is short. As such, it makes the students' reading task and the teacher's coverage easier. Second, it is universal. Students all over the world have experienced stories and can relate to them. Third and most important, short fiction, like all literature, contributes to the development of cognitive analytical abilities, bringing the whole self to bear on a compressed account of a situation in a single place and moment. Focused and memorable, it is an essential part of the language and cultural experience available to ESL students. Potter (1983) presents additional creative and useful reasons for the study of fiction for nonnative speakers.

The Main Aspects of Short Fiction in ESL

Archibald MacLeish (b. 1892), an American poet and dramatist, once wrote in a poem called "Ars Poetica" that "a poem should not mean but be" (1982). What he meant, at least on one level, was that a poem in itself should and does convey meaning not by what it states in words, sentences, and so on, but by virtue of its existence and overall impression on the reader. This idea also applies to short fiction because short story writers aim to make as strong an immediate impact, a single impression, as possible and involve the reader as rapidly as possible. A story thus has its own reason for being--to involve the reader. "Powerhouse is playing!" writes American author Eudora Welty (1966, p. 523) in the first sentence of the short story "Powerhouse," and readers are immediately engaged in the activity of the present continuous, intransitive verb *playing*. They want to know the who, what, where, when, and how of *playing* and why it is important. The story, barely begun by the reader, already exists and exerts control over the imagination.

How do ESL students react when studying short fiction? Of course, they may experience, as with poetry, some fear of the work itself. They may feel it is too difficult for them. This, however, is not their sole reaction. Unlike their response to poetry, with fiction they often react more directly and more strongly to the subject matter, that is, to the story line itself. The story line produces in them a strong reaction for or against the tale itself. That is, they often react against the subject of the story, the events, rather than the message the author conveys through the story. They may not await the content. This may also occur with poetry, but since poems usually have a less obvious story line, the particular student reaction to it is not as frequent.

One additional factor among many is that students are simply more familiar with storytelling and listening than they are with poetry. They have heard stories, in the form of anecdotes, folk and fairy tales, and other narratives, all their lives. Because they are already familiar with the concept of the story line, they feel more comfortable with stories and freer to react spontaneously to them, both positively and negatively. The story, like all literary forms, is unique and requires unique strategies for understanding.

Although the study of a story may begin at any point in it, the student's level of familiarity with the form is an important factor in determining the best entry point after the initial reading. The student's first contact with the story, after grasping the plot, is significant because the students may aleady have a strong, perhaps negative, initial reaction to the surface. Thus the first aspect of a short story to be discussed must be enough of a catalyst that students who are put off by the surface will still want to continue on toward the story's center.

Carefully choose the corridor by which you enter a story, asking yourself whether the character you intend to discuss, the action you plan to focus on, or the conflict you wish to explore will stimulate the students sufficiently to be willing to leave behind the comfortable clarity of plot for the density of interpretation. As a starting point, students may create a list of questions that provide a departure from the story line.

What are the communication essentials of an effective short story for ESL students? They are surely not identical to those used with a story intended for literary study by native English-speaking graduate students or teachers of literature. The ESL teacher must consider whether the story's components can and will with proper explanation facilitate the student-reader's entrance into and experience of the narrative. Another criterion is that of the evocation of student interest in the story. Does a particular element of short fiction writing act as a catalyst for the student to read on in the story and seek out more fiction?

Of course, the significant elements of the craft of fiction, as of poetry, differ from work to work. Obviously, not all elements are equally prominent in all works. Still, Stephen Crane's fictionalized account of an autobiographical experience, "The Open Boat" (1897) in Stallman (1955), contains the communication essentials in a story appropriate for nonnative readers. This tale can serve as a model of a story that is fully accessible to and broadly useful for such students.

"The Open Boat" is widely perceived as appropriate for nonnative students. In their classification of some American literary works, Harris and Harris (1967) declared the 3,000- to 4,000-word level effective for the low-advanced level. They limited their criteria to vocabulary, saying they had developed no accurate way to evaluate grammatical and structural appropriateness. Some students may indeed find the style of "The Open Boat" difficult (to be discussed later), but the clarity of its other communication essentials--structure, theme, voice, language, and character--provide a strong base from which students can build an understanding of Crane's style. The story itself, moreover, concerning the 27-hour ordeal of men faced with the relatively unfamiliar, a shipwreck and possible death, is set in a familiar context, the sea. It embodies Crane's belief that no one can interpret life without first experiencing it, mirroring many nonnative students' experiences, thus appealing to them.

Plot should be inherently interesting. The quantity of action may not be as crucial as its quality. Quality depends on the story's capacity to engage and hold the reader. Plot, in this sense, means not only definite actions but structured progression toward a resolution. In "The Open Boat," this progression includes the remarks of the men in the boat as their hopes rise and fall; a seagull amazing the captain by landing on his head; the movement of seaweed around the boat; and so on. Within the context of the shipwrecked men's plight at sea, the action is vigorous and yet not so busy that it confuses the reader. And, as in most stories, the plot emanates from a central conflict or seemingly unresolvable problem. Techniques for demonstrating this basic aspect of the short story will be discussed later. While plot by itself often serves to attract readers, it may become confusing or boring, and quickly cause readers to lose interest. To sustain the plot's hold on the reader, to ensure that it remains clear to the reader, as well as to establish a clear time frame and a vivid, recognizable setting, an effective structure is essential.

Structure

While the complexity and intensity of a story's events, its scenario, usually pose no special problems for ESL students, an unclear structure may cause difficulty. A clear yet dynamic structure has the greatest power either to attract or to repel students' attention at the outset of studying a story.

The structure of "The Open Boat" is both dynamic and lucid. In the opening paragraphs, the characters are introduced and presented to the reader in the familiar terms of their worldly occupations and in terms of their present positions in the boat. This categorization is reinforced soon after at the start of Section III: "They were a captain, an oiler, a cook, and a correspondent, and they were friends--friends in a more curiously iron-bound degree than may be common" (p. 220). After introducing the characters, Crane photographs them continually from various angles and at various time intervals. These snapshots serve as the story's first major structural device.

The men's alternating hopes and fears are the basis of the second structure. As the land approaches and recedes, or seems to do so from their vantage point, they are either elated or dejected. These ups and downs balance the tale. At one point, the seemingly static seaweed informs "the men in the boat that it [the boat] was making progress slowly toward the land" (p. 219). The land itself looms "slowly and beautifully" (p. 219) out of the sea. Inspired by the sight of the lighthouse, the men hope rescuers will soon appear. But as night comes on: "The shore grew dusky. The man waving a coat blended gradually into this gloom, and it swallowed in the same manner the omnibus and the group of people" (p. 229). At intervals, the reader's attention is called to the rise and fall of the men's hopes, a discernible and dramatic pattern that holds the story together.

Repetition, parallelism, and variation of statements, both of fact and of feeling, act as a third formal device. Within the framework of a seven-part structure, the nature of the sea is revealed, including the disadvantage that "lies in the fact that after successfully surmounting one wave, you discover that there is another behind it just as important and just as nervously anxious to do something effective in the way of swamping boats" (p. 216). Earlier, the reader was told that "The manner of her scramble over these walls of water is a mystic thing" (p. 216). Later, it is reported that the boat's progress despite its vicious splashing by the crests is nothing less than a miracle: "She seemed like a wee thing wallowing, miraculously top up, at the mercy of five oceans" (p. 220). The following statement seems to be the culmination of all, but, like the waves, it is simply another restatement of the flux that is Crane's focus:

> As each slaty wall of water approached, it shut all else from the view of the men in the boat, and it was not difficult to imagine that this particular wave was the final outburst of the ocean, the last effort of the grim water. There was a terrible grace in the move of the waves, and they came in silence, save for the snarling of the crests. (p. 216)

Amid the flurry and apparent chaos of the sea and of the men's thoughts, Crane offers these reports on the regular motion of the waves as structural handles for readers to grasp as the story advances. The statements periodically reorient the reader to the steady attempt of the men to make headway against the sea in order to reach the shore. Readers are reminded that they are reading and witnessing an account of a journey that has signposts and demarcations, even if they are only the changing motion of the waves.

The alternation of the men's sometimes frenzied and anxious dialogue with an apparently detached narrator is another formal device that may be observed. The two extremes serve to balance the central concern: Will the boat and its crew make it to shore? The narrator is often noncommittal: "Shipwrecks are apropos of nothing. If men could only train for them and have them occur when the men had reached pink condition, there would be less drowning at sea" (pp. 221-222). In Section IV, the men vigorously debate exactly what they think they see:

> "What the devil is that thing?"
> "Why, it looks like a boat."
> "Why, certainly, it's a boat."
> "No; it's on wheels."
> "Yes, so it is. Well, that must be the life-boat. They drag them along shore on a wagon."
> "That's the life-boat, sure."
> "No, by God, it's--it's an omnibus."
> "I tell you it's a life-boat" (p. 227).

But the narrator, still removed, remarks: "It is fair to say here that there was not a life-saving station within twenty miles in either direction; but the men did not know this fact, and in consequence they made dark and opprobrious remarks concerning the eyesight of the nation's life-savers" (p. 224). The consistent opposition of these two points of view is a structural underpinning guiding the reader as the four-man crew seeks favorable winds.

Reinforcing and yet superseding these formal aspects of "The Open Boat" is the incantatory power infused throughout the story. It is so familiar and so immediately compelling to readers that it seems to be an organic part of the story rather than an artifice of the author. "If I am going to be drowned--if I am going to be drowned," the speaker insists, why was I taken this far merely to have my nose dragged away as I was about to nibble the sacred cheese of life?" (p. 224). It is chanted twice more, once in Section IV and a final time in Section VI: "If I am going to be drowned--if I am going to be drowned--if I am going to be drowned--why, in the name of the seven mad gods who rule the sea, was I allowed to come thus far and contemplate sand and trees?" (p. 232). No definite answer is ever given--only the comment from a human perspective that the predicament seems "an abominable injustice indeed" (p. 233). Yet, the question itself, raised to a higher and higher pitch as the men prepare to make the inevitable run at the shore, assumes increasing importance. As the struggle reaches a climax, the question takes on a dynamic structural value.

Theme

The concept of culture shock offers a lens through which to view an individual's uprooting from his or her home culture, traversing time and space and entering a new zone. Most nonnative students experience a basic disorientation while living outside their own countries. In "The Open Boat," Crane studies the symptoms of such disorientation. The major motifs of the story, including the journey motif, are offshoots of his interest in it.

What direction are we taking? What journey are we embarking on? Where are we going? These are the questions the men of the story ask themselves and Nature. The "immovable quality" (p. 238) of the shore is both a solace and a frustration to them, offering evidence that a destination does exist, but defying the notion that it is reachable. Out of this first theme emerge several other themes, all concerned with perceptions of oneself and one's fellows caught in the same situation.

The universal rule of "women and children first" is an interesting frame of reference in this situation, where there are no women or children, and no boat to put them in anyway even if they were present. About whom is one or should one be concerned in such a situation? The conflict between the essence of camaraderie on the one hand and sharp, pure concern for self on the other is vividly shaped. It shows itself in the disbelief the men experience when they find that they are not seen by people on shore whom they can see, and who seem to be going about their business normally. Here the men's joy is in imagining that the man on shore is really waving at them. They wonder, how can we not be seen? How can we not be important? The conflict extends to their past experiences also, a past in which the correspondent had read a poem about a dying soldier. It hadn't mattered to him back then. Now he sees it as a "human, living thing" and "was sorry for the soldier of the Legion who lay dying in Algiers" (p. 234). Concern for self, for survival, compels people to consider their concern both for themselves and for others. In Crane's vision, the matter is not only considered, but reconsidered and reevaluated.

Of course, wondering whether others are thinking of us is only a short distance from wondering whether Nature itself is concerned about its creatures, one of Crane's most important themes in this story and in all his work. In a touching moment, the voyagers, beset by waves, cold, dark, and fear, admit in an outburst, "'Yes, but I love myself'" (p. 233). Glimpsing later that other humans may not notice them or care, that nature itself may be "flatly indifferent" (p. 236), they determine their course. After a conference among the four, the Captain decides, "If no help is coming, we might better try a run through the surf right away. If we stay out here much longer we will be too weak to do anything for ourselves at all" (p. 236). He states the motive or condition for action clearly: If nobody or nothing, including Nature, cares about us, then we had better take care of ourselves. To Crane, Nature's uninterest in her creatures seems all the stranger because she has imbued them with so much concern ("love") for themselves.

While Crane suggests no resolution to this dilemma, he does imply, in another theme, that experience and the understanding that comes from it can help people comprehend. The experience of wrestling with the sea has forced the men to review the case. While they have not had time or the leisure to reconsider what their new understanding means, they know that they must begin to see their world differently. Although they cannot specify exactly how, a few random images of changed behavior come to their minds: "He understands that if he were given another opportunity, he would mend his conduct and his words, and be better and brighter during an introduction or at a tea" (pp. 236-237). Experience--especially the experience of possible or likely death--makes a difference. Such experience enables people to see the world of the shore--the familiar world--and the world of the sea--the unfamiliar world--in a different light. It encourages a different perspective, not necessarily positive, but decidedly new. Moreover, it teaches people not to take their own assumptions too seriously. Loss of connections to time and place can make the unfamiliar seem familiar, and the familiar--even home--seem utterly unrecognizable.

Voice

If theme engages nonnative students, then rich, contextualized narrative voices can entice and hold them. To get students to accurately receive, respond to, and be able to imitate the voices contextualized in a clear setting is, of course, one of the main goals of most language instruction for nonnative speakers. "The Open Boat" has no dearth of strong, contrasting voices serving as highly graphic models of voices in authentic situations. Beneath the varied voices, of course, Crane has chosen a point of view or speaker. As in a poem, the speaker and the author are not necessarily the same person. Crane has selected a point of view or, in this instance, shifting points of view appropriate to the context. He examines events from the minds of the rowers, from those on shore, and from a semidetached, somewhat unidentifiable narrator. Each has a distinctive voice of his or her own, and each reacts to the events using this voice.

Thus Crane places the reader at once in a real, and threatening, situation. From the start, readers experience the sweep of the waves. As the story continues, a variety of voices maintains their involvement in the events. At times, readers are distanced from the men, able only to speculate about their feelings: "The faces of the men must have been grey" (pp. 216-217). At other times, they are embodied in their thoughts: "If she has decided to drown me, why did she not do it in the beginning and save me all this trouble?" (pp. 224-225). The movement switches back from involvement to distant observer again when a voice observes: "It may be remarked that a man would conclude that it was really the intention of the seven mad gods to drown him, despite the abominable injustice of it" (pp. 232-233). All voices, involved and detached, character and authorial, seem equally strong. The result is a tension between contrasting voices of equal power, tugging readers this way and that, each vying for our allegiance without gaining and holding it, each an absolutely clear call in an instantly comprehensible situation.

Language

The language Crane uses is his most penetrating communication device in "The Open Boat." His masterful use of language is not a matter of vocabulary or style but one of figurative language: idioms, images, sounds, all conducive to context analysis but not dependent on glossing for comprehension. Crane's language can be understood, of course; more important, it can easily be absorbed and appreciated. Its richness, rather than impeding the reader's understanding, gives it clarity and impact. Its richness challenges at the same time as it communicates.

The dominant language clusters in the story are animals; colors; and two of the four elements, fire and water. The contest between the men and the sea is reinforced with language from the wild. The boat--prancing, rearing, plunging--is like an animal: "As each wave came, and she rose for it, she seemed like a horse making at a fence outrageously high" (p. 216). On the other hand, the birds that approach the boat are uncomfortable and perceive the sea as would "a covey of prairie chickens a thousand miles inland" (p. 218). A seagull attacks the captain's head. It is difficult to move about in such a boat, more difficult than "to steal eggs from under a hen" (p. 219). Can this "wild colt" of a craft actually manage against the "mountain cat" waves? (pp. 223-224). In language of the animal world, crisp and clear to all, Crane poses but does not answer this final question.

Color is the backdrop against which the men's struggles occur. "None of them knew the colour of the sky," the story begins (p. 215). The time of day is indicated also by color: "They knew it was broad day because the color of the sea changed from slate to emerald green streaked with amber lights. . . . The process of the breaking day was unknown to them. They were aware only of this effect upon the colour of the waves that rolled toward them" (p. 217). Color is the only concrete, solid manifestation of the world about them, from the "white lip of a wave as it spun up the beach," to a tiny house "blocked out black upon the sky," to the "grey length" of a "slim lighthouse" (p. 223). Objects don't have but assume color, and land seems "but a long black shadow on the sea"

(p. 221). When it becomes distinct, it becomes "a line of black and a line of white" (p. 222).

All changes or apparent changes in the men's perceptions are recorded in terms of color, as if this is the most distinct measure possible in such a situation. The passage of time, difficult to perceive in a boat, is measured by light: "A night on the sea in an open boat is a long night. As darkness settled finally, the shine of the light, lifting from the sea in the south, changed to full gold. On the northern horizon a new light appeared, a small bluish gleam on the edge of the waters. These two lights were the furniture of the world. Otherwise, there was nothing but waves" (p. 230). Light is not only the start and culmination of each stage of this journey, but the only "absolute," even as it shifts, in this universe of no absolutes.

Crane combines the language of color with its natural offshoot, the language of heat and cold. Sometimes these extremes are tied to their natural associations; at other times, they are connected unnaturally to their opposites. The ocean, though known finally by the men as cold, nearly swamps the boat "like white flames" (p. 220). The sunlight "flamed on the tips of the waves" (p. 236). A "high cold star" is the only response the correspondent can discover to his love for himself. There is a watch fire on the beach, but it is too far off to emit any heat for the rowers. The heat and cold of the elements intertwine as they play across the men's eyes, ears, and skins.

The language of animal movement, color perception, and sensitivity to heat and cold, familiar to all human beings, pervades the story and serves to remind all, native and nonnative alike, of the universality of these elements and of everyone's connectedness to them.

Character

Intimate, visceral understanding of the characters in a story allows readers to penetrate the story and respond fully to it. Complex, growing, changing characters involve people and elicit their compassion on the one hand or disdain on the other. Threatened with extinction, Crane's characters in "The Open Boat" evoke empathy. With the familiar world of the shore visible but unobtainable to them, they row toward it in the midst of a sea nearly as familiar to them as land but now unfamiliarly dangerous. Crane--or a narrator--tugs the reader into their plight at once with his statement that "Many a man ought to have a bathtub larger than the boat which here rode upon the sea" (p. 215). With this reference to a convenience found in most homes, Crane calls on readers to empathize with the four men trapped in an even tinier space. Readers ask themselves, inevitably: "How would I feel so enclosed? How would I feel being in sight of something familiar yet still in danger of extinction?" So challenged, readers become involved: "Is this my world?" they ask. "Is it as familiar and as safe as it seems?"

Character and plot, of course, overlap. Characters rarely make an impact on a reader unless the plot is also striking. If the situation, the plight of the characters, is durable, readers can visualize it long after they leave it. "The Open Boat" pulls readers away from their safe positions and makes them sit with the cook, the oiler, the captain, and the correspondent--those antipilgrims--as they face heat, cold, sharks, and wave after wave. Readers lose the sureness of their step and experience the true fragility of the world, and how it fluctuates. Readers remember not only the sea's movement, but the fluctuations, the rhythms, of the men's hopes as they see the shore and the people on it draw close and then recede. This flux, reinforced by structure, rich narrative voices, and lush varied images, is memorable.

The essential aspects of a story are certainly not limited to the five discussed here. Any full discussion of a tale should also take into account factors such as the pace or speed of the narrative, its tone, significant symbols, and style, just to name a few. Furthermore, in a particular story, any of these factors may be more important than the five discussed here. Each story is a separate case, requiring a unique judgment of the factors that will contribute most to understanding.

Criteria for Selecting Stories

When selecting stories to present to ESL students, the elements of conflict, plot, and style should be considered carefully. The plot or conflict should be looked at in the light of its (a) comprehensibility and (b) the cultural attitudes of the target audience. If the plot contains too many circumlocutions, this fact, combined with other difficulties the ESL student may be experiencing, could drive the student away. The plot, simply stated, should be both interesting and not too difficult to follow. When it is not, efforts should be made to help students deal with it. Further, the plot should not be so foreign or unfamiliar culturally--or so offensive--to students that they are repelled by it. While the broadest possible choice of subject matter should be made for short fiction, it is unfortunate to allow some subject to come between a student and the rich genre of short fiction.

Similarly, the literary style a student first encounters may have lasting harmful effects. If a student must confront several pages of a style that he or she has difficulty processing, the experience of short story reading in general may simply seem too arduous to overcome.

Again, the question of what constitutes difficult prosodic style is complex. The style of "The Open Boat," made up of mostly Subject-Verb-Object sentences, is not inherently difficult. The following passage is one of the more complex:

> The sun swung steadily up the sky, and they knew it was broad day because the color of the sea changed from slate to emerald-green streaked with amber lights, and the foam was like tumbling snow. The process of the breaking day was unknown to them. They were aware only of this effect upon the color of the waves that rolled toward them. (p. 217)

The level of detail and the complex syntax may discourage readers. However, it is essential to recognize that such a style impedes readers only if the teacher allows it to do so. For example, the preceding passage need not and should not be tackled when the class first begins studying the story. It can wait, without limiting comprehension, until a later stage of study. It may not even be necessary to read this passage at all. The story can be grasped without it. Second, the passage may be made more comprehensible by drawing attention to the parallel sentences. Another technique is to have groups of students work together on selected sentences and then explain them to the entire class. The question of the need for full comprehension of a text is fully discussed in the section on selecting literary materials. It should be noted here that the facilitator should carefully consider an author's style before assigning his or her work to students.

"The Open Boat" can help prepare students for difficulties with style. Topping (1968) insists that "Our students are much more likely to want to read of the Pueblo [the ship involved in a 1965 attack leading to the war in Vietnam] rather than "The Open Boat..." or that "this is the America all students need to know" (p. 100). However, no literature dictates such a choice. A story is communicative by virtue of being a paradigm of life, and even when life seems remote from the story, the story encourages students to enter its realm.

Having briefly considered these two important criteria for selecting stories, it is now appropriate to look at some less technical considerations of the selection process.

Stories penetrate students' consciousness and lives to the extent that they correlate usefully and appealingly with those lives. An effective story has *communicative power*. This phrase suggests that the story presents a situation replete with words, real or symbolic gestures, nuances, and acts that students can recognize, use, or envision using in daily life. Obviously, students will not need to learn how to row a boat off the Florida coast; but they will experience bad weather, shifts in plans, and both hope and despair. They will have to know how to think about the future, even how to question the present. They will need to consider their own or another person's approaching death.

A well-crafted story such as "The Open Boat" will also draw readers and communicate with them through its inherent qualities and its potential to evoke associations. In addition, such a story often contains the potential to prompt many reader activities that reinforce grammatical and syntactic skills. "The Open Boat" is especially rich in such benefits.

The structure of the story, while clear and stimulating, is by no means the only structure possible. People from other cultures may view the dynamic differently and may enjoy envisioning a different order. Asking them to rearrange the events of the plot will elicit some of these cultural differences. They may especially wish to vary the ending. They may not find it plausible or natural that only one person survives, for example. Their outlines of the structure, presented to the whole class, can serve as an impetus for discussion. The powerful auditory aspect of the tale can stimulate students to record on cassette tape or in their writing similar spoken voices they hear outside the classroom. Moreover, they can draw on Crane's pictorial power by sketching scenes from the story, conveying clearly the visual effect they received. They can also role play parts of the story, taking on the personalities of one or another character. Each student may be asked to pick a difficult word, sentence, image, character, or scene and become an expert on it, explaining it and its role in the story to the group, using it as an entry point to the story. The same can be done with the author's biography. Each student may bring in one piece of information about the author's life, and the class may piece together a brief, composite biography. Discussion and debate emerging from these exercises will enable the students to look carefully at questions of justice, individual human capacity, and other such matters.

Stephen Crane's "The Open Boat" points the way for short story instructors in an ESL context. Teachers and students need not fear the apparently complex. Teachers should simply choose their favorite stories and begin to teach them. Discover, as with poetry, which aspects (characters, vocabulary, etc.) you can most easily ask questions about. Divide and conquer: ask one group of students to discuss one character and another group to handle a different character. Then bring their observations in contact with each other. do not attempt to swallow any whole story or even several aspects of a story in a brief session, especially at first. This approach, especially with stories like "The Open Boat," but even with those that may require rereading, allows readers to become "interpreters" of language, culture, and even life. By teaching stories whole, substituting knowledge, confidence, and teaching skill for cutting, abridging, rewriting, or overglossing the story, teachers help nonnative speakers find their way in a strange environment and consider their places vis-à-vis the culture's mainstream.

Model Worksheet for "The Open Boat"

I. Background

A Man Said to the Universe
A man said to the universe:
"Sir, I exist!"
"However," replied the universe,
"The fact has not created in me
A sense of obligation."

(Crane, 1981, p. 1241)

1. Read the preceding poem. Identify the attitude Crane is expressing. Which character, if any, in "The Open Boat" expresses a similar view?

2. Crane experienced and wrote a news story about the events of the story. He even spoke to the ship's captain after writing the story to verify the authenticity of the details. Does this influence your view of the story? Why or why not?

II. Plot and Structure

1. Is there anything not included in the story that you would have liked to know about the events? If it were included, would the story be a better story? Discuss.

Teaching Short Stories

2. Do you like and agree with the story's conclusion? Why or why not?

III. Pace, Length, Style

1. Is the story too long? If so, what should be omitted?

2. Do the words of the story give you a clear picture of the men's plight? Consider the italicized words in the following sentences and replace them with words you might have used.

   a. The craft *pranced* and *reared* and *plunged* like an animal.
   b. Many a man ought to have a *bathtub* larger than the boat which here rose upon the sea.
   c. The coldness of the water was *sad;* it was tragic.
   d. She (Nature) did not seem cruel to him, then, nor beneficient, nor treacherous, nor wise. But she was indifferent, flatly *indifferent*.

IV. Character

1. Which character do you most sympathize with? Least? Why?

2. Retell part of the tale from another (a person on shore, a helicopter pilot, the water, or the boat) point of view. How does it change?

V. Theme and Tone

1. Is the story tragic? You may first compare it with similar narratives: Lawrence Sergent Hall's (1915-) "The Ledge," William Gilbert's (1836-1911) "The Yarn of the Nancy Bell," or Jack London's (1876-1916) "To Build a Fire."

2. How would the people in your country be likely to react on hearing this tale?

VI. Visual View

Sketch the final scene. What would compose the foreground? Background? Explain.

Principles for Teaching Fiction in the ESL Setting

First, use the inherent power and natural flow of the story itself as a guide to teaching it. Determine which aspects of the story will provide the most enjoyment and yield the greatest learning. A story like "The Open Boat" responds best to an examination of language or of structure. Other stories may benefit from a metaphorical apparoach. Vary your choice of aspects of the story to emphasize according to the nature of the story itself. Some aspects may have more weight in one story than in another. A first reading of the story will reveal a character, a place, or a particular use of language that stands out. Follow up on this aspect.

Second, identify and draw in students' past experiences through telling and listening. Because the story is universal, students from all cultures have surely had some experience with it. Ask students to tell about their experiences with stories, both to make them more comfortable with them and to give you a better sense of what they know and do not know about them. You can then incorporate the essential elements that students are already able to describe, especially at the beginning of the semester. Their early understanding will provide an excellent foundation for an understanding of narrative and will be a useful frame of reference throughout the term.

Third, encourage students to seek and observe interconnections between aspects of the story. Both teachers and students tend to hone in on an area of the story with which they feel familiar, at the expense of other aspects. In general, encourage students to explore the whole story and infer intelligently from one aspect to another rather than trying to draw conclusions from isolated aspects. This approach is especially important in a student's first reading of a story. Henderson (1983) rightly warns that "compartmentalizing story units . . . should be avoided" and recommends a holistic approach to pursue the goal of "total story appreciation" (p. 14).

Fourth, provide preparatory background before approaching difficult vocabulary and allusion. ESL teachers are generally agreed that students need some help with vocabulary and unfamiliar allusions. But the degree of help necessary is sometimes a matter of debate, as well as the best way to provide it--through developing vocabulary attack skills or by glossing. In the preparation of literary materials for ESL students, glossing is a frequent solution. Povey (1979) suggests ways for teachers to determine whether they are glossing appropriately (the words students really do not know) and sufficiently (all the words the students need to know).

The amount of cultural background information necessary is more difficult to specify. Marckwardt (1978) raises the question of "whether the acquisition of a considerable degree of competence in the language should imply the acquisition of a second culture as well" (p. 47). While he does not answer the question directly, he mentions that among the bilingual people he has known, "I doubt that anyone of them could realistically be described as bicultural" (p. 47). While most would agree that some cultural preparation is necessary before students take on a complicated story by themselves, a problem remains. Povey (1979) explains that a student "who can readily recognize unfamiliar words is far less likely to know what will prove to be a cultural difficulty since s/he is so often unable to recognize its individuality" (p. 173). Moreover it is difficult to detect which cultural elements students are not grasping accurately. One solution, while not a perfect one, is the middle ground: provide necessary cultural background in advance, and clear up additional cultural questions as they arise. As the ability to do so may not come naturally, teacher training programs must show teachers how to fill in students' cultural gaps.

Fifth, guide the students concerning how and when to read a story. After tackling the problem of gaps in nonnative readers' vocabulary and cultural knowledge, teachers may consider timing a minor matter. Yet it is of great importance. While most poems are short enough to read aloud in class, short fiction usually is not. Still, selected portions of a tale can be usefully read aloud to provide an introduction to the story and to help students get a grasp of it. Povey (1979) suggests that students do two readings of the story on their own, first for a general understanding and then to grapple with the interpretation and understanding of larger meanings. Other possibilities include reading aloud with accompanying pictures (Reese, 1979) or reading the bulk of a longer work, such as a novel, in translation as well as major parts in the original (Marckwardt, 1978).

Sixth, be sure that everyone has a clear understanding of the story line and of the basic reltionships among the characters. Frequently, a teacher is surprised midway or even further into a lesson on a short story to find that one or more students do not know that a character is a relative of another character or that a particular event has taken place. Nonnative readers of short fiction may overlook or not comprehend the meaning of a remark that refers to an essential relationship or plot segment. Therefore, instructors must ensure through questioning, or asking students to paraphrase portions of the story, that every student has a clear and full understanding of the story line and the interrelationships among characters. This basic step should be completed early in the discussion of a story.

Seventh, define literary terms as necessary to facilitate student discussion. These can be found in easily available dictionaries of literary terms. Translate the terms into language nonnative readers can understand, and familiarize students with these essential terms as necessary, providing examples in stories they are reading. The term *point of view*, for example, is simply an efficient way of quickly identifying the narrative angle of a story. Students will probably not need to know all literary nomenclature, but the knowledge of a few useful terms can simplify discussion.

Eighth, demonstrate the poetic side of short fiction. Although the essential element in short fiction is a dynamic story line, much short fiction is not without its poetical side. Many a short fiction writer's style--think of Eudora Welty, Ralph Ellison, and Frank O'Connor--is notable for its poetry. And, of course, writers who are not especially noted for their poetic abilities sometimes need to create a poetic passage for a fictional purpose. The poetry of fiction is best discovered by reading passages aloud. In this way stories' music will reveal itself.

Ninth, enjoy reading and discussing short fiction. While learning is important in teaching fiction to ESL students, enjoyment is the goal. These two aims are not distinct: when a student learns a great deal about a story, he or she has undoubtedly enjoyed the process.

In addition to these guidelines, many other principles for teaching literature in an ESL context may be followed. Povey (1984) provides excellent guidelines, covering preclass preparation, in-class work, first appraisal of a story, and cross-cultural discussion. Povey (1979) suggests that the most convenient approach to a story is through its characters. Indeed, character provides direct access to a story. He also illustrates a method for drawing students into a story through questions, doing great justice to the subtlety that effective questioning requires. "One's speculations," he writes, "must be translated into questions one can also ask the students. For some classes these queries may go too far, too fast. When one fails to elicit responses immediately, one should go back into the more comfortable area of factual questions with which one began" (pp. 176-177).

Of course, principles are no substitute for observing actual classroom sessions. Povey (1979) presents an account of a treatment of a Willa Cather tale, similar to the discussion here of "The Open Boat." It is in classrooms that teachers can more easily observe the pleasure students experience when they discuss a story they have read. Such pleasure is similar to the pleasure first experienced reading the story, a "sensual and intellectual pleasure," writes Charters (1983) "that results when you begin to understand its individual magic" (p. 17).

Classroom Activities Following Discussion of a Short Story

Short stories have an automatic impact on their readers. Instructors may extend this impact through activities growing out of the stories. Lively activities serve to reinforce students' understanding of the story, to help them remember it, and to show them that it can lead to still more knowledge and greater enjoyment.

Activities connected with short fiction usually aim toward definite learning objectives for the students. These objectives include reinforcing or reviewing grammatical points; developing vocabulary; improving students' organizational skills; increasing students' knowledge of the target culture; interpreting the literature in the conventional sense; and simply helping the students enjoy the story. Activities sometimes focus first on eliminating language problems, often acute in nonnative readers, and then on aspects that are not specifically of interest to nonnative readers and are taught in many native reader literature courses.

One kind of activity using short fiction that is equally applicable to both native and nonnative readers is so basic that many overlook it. Before presenting a short story, prepare for it with another very short work by the same author. Or use quotations from an interview, if available, with the author. In the case of Stephen Crane's "The Open Boat," the facilitator may introduce the author and the story with one of Crane's brief poems such as "A Man Said to the Universe." The brief introduction and discussion of a short, usually more readily comprehensible, work by the same author may relax the students and, by providing some background in a miniature context, ease their task of understanding the longer, more complex target work. The shorter work need not be completely discussed; its sole function is to introduce the author's style and themes.

Many activities centering on short fiction are designed to review and improve selected areas of students' grammatical capacities. The emphasis is and should be on the students' ability to correct and improve any remaining grammatical weaknesses on their own with little guidance. By the time students reach high intermediate or advanced ESL courses, they have usually mastered many of the essential structures and functions. Often lagging behind are matters such as formulating more sophisticated and more structurally complex questions; control of tenses and time sequence; the ability to combine sentences emphatically and fluently; and other areas. These, and, of course, the goal of grammatical flexibility--the ability to maneuver language elements with ease and verve--should be the focus of activities done in conjunction with fiction.

Beyond the models that short fiction automatically provides, what activities can achieve these objectives? McConochie (1975) illustrates a way in which students can improve their control of syntax through fiction. First they divide sentences into shorter sentences. Then, without consulting the original sentences, they recombine the smaller sentences and compare the result with the original. Waldinger (1980) suggests another rewarding exercise: have students rewrite parts of a story in another tense. He also suggests using *when* and synchronizing past tenses to point up cause-and-effect relationships. Many variations on this technique are possible. Rewriting sentences that have no subject or verb into complete sentences, as suggested by McConochie (1975), will help students gain full control over formulating questions and other sentence types. The questions will be natural contextual questions at that. Oller (1983) recommends storytelling, still a viable activity.

Any activity should remain fairly close to the original story. Each activity asks the students to accomplish a task that is not merely a mechanical exercise. If done properly, each activity simultaneously enables the student to improve his or her grammar and learn something more about the story itself. The value of an activity can certainly be judged by the degree to which it fosters such growth.

Fiction rarely uses bland language. It depends on a rich mixture and varied levels of word usage. Thus it affords students an opportunity to increase their vocabulary and their sensitivity to and appreciation of words. Although Anglo-Saxon writers called their vocabulary their word-hoard, short fiction writers do not hoard their words at all. The rich array of idioms and sensory evocations found in short fiction is a sweet, pleasant blend students can savor. Consider the second paragraph of Welty's (1966) story, "Powerhouse":

> He's here on tour from the city--"Powerhouse and His Keyboard"--"Powerhouse and His Tasmanians"--think of the things he calls himself! There's no one in the world like him. You can't tell what he is. "Nigger man"?--he looks more Asiatic, monkey, Jewish, Babylonian, Peruvian, fanatic, devil. He has pale gray eyes when they're open. He has African feet of the greatest size, stomping, both together, on each side of the pedals. He's not coal black--beverage colored--looks like a preacher when his mouth is shut, but then it opens--vast and obscene. And his mouth is going every minute: like a monkey's when it looks for something. Improvising, coming on a light and childish melody--*smooch*--he loves it with his mouth. (p. 523)

Equally metaphorical passages can be found in many other short stories, from Joyce's "Araby" to Katherine Anne Porter's "Maria Concepción."

What should the teacher do with this resource--vocabulary? Much more can be done besides explaining the words, although this will sometimes be necessary. Recognizing and being able to point out denotation and positive and negative connotations are important skills, as Mullen (1984) vividly demonstrates with phrases from Angelica Gibbs' short story, "The Test." Students are asked to label words as denotative or positively or negatively connotative. More knowledge of and facility with synonyms and antonyms, McConochie (1975) suggests, can develop from working with the language of a short story. Black English and its unique use of language is the subject of Schlepper's (1979) work on a story by Dudley Randall. Translation exercises from black English to standard English, also included in Mullen (1984), while a well-intentioned suggestion, may leave the nonnative reader with a pejorative view of the former because it suggests that black English needs to be translated to standard English in order to be understood. For a vigorous and healthier activity, ask the student-readers to retell a story, in pairs or individually, several times, gradually increasing the complexity of the language (Bradford, 1968). Here word recognition and vocabulary development merge.

Indeed, all these activities ask nonnative readers of short stories to get involved with stories and delve into the stories' words.

At the high intermediate level and especially at the advanced level, the teacher seeks to firm up the nonnative student's ability to organize his or her thoughts in English. Here the teacher encourages the student to achieve complete control over central and supporting ideas, as well as various supporting details, of a story. If the ordering and linking of parcels of thought is, like most language and thinking tasks, culturally relative, then the options available in English will still not be fully familiar to most students. They will need exposure to structural options. Once again, short fiction can help.

Short fiction writers, like all writers, stake out their time and space, carefully placing events in both. They distribute actions and incidents across both frames in various unique ways. These typical working practices of short story writers easily lend themselves to various activities focusing on story organization. During the presentation and discussion of the story, the instructor should lead students to observe the various structures used to contain the elements of tales. Observing such models, the students will be able to transfer these and other patterns in an appropriate way to their own writings. Moreover, class activities go beyond mere osmosis, transfer, and imitation. Students can and should be asked to take part in and accomplish pertinent activities.

One useful activity is to compile a chart of opposite or opposing elements in a story, concretizing the conflicts and struggles that are the essence of a good story. Students can modify the ending of the tale or even invent a new one, discussing the effects alternate endings would have on the story as a whole and on the reader. They can retell the story, as DiPietro (1982) suggests, tuning in to various options the author may have used at strategic points. They can and should distinguish between primary and secondary events in the plot. They could even draw a map of the geographical movement of the story (White, 1977). Carrying this task a step further, students may make a full drawing of the motion--another word for order--of the story. The benefits of such organizational activities and the many other possibilities scholars have suggested and teachers can create include, at the very least: (a) a clearer understanding of the story in question; (b) an improved ability to decipher patterns in all the reading they do; and (c) an enhanced appreciation of the short story's riches.

The authors and narrators of stories arrange themselves into an infinitely long caravan of voices--some ironic, some sensitive, still others seductive, and so on. What better way for the high intermediate and advanced ESL student to discover his or her own voice in English than by listening to these many varieties? Such authentic voices far surpass the usual dialogues, which, as Hilferty and Lezberg (1979) have said, "are frequently contextualized minimally or not at all proportionate to their relative importance to the total syllabus" (p. 49). Others, such as Widdowson (1982), have made the same point. The human voice in short fiction is, on the contrary, always contextualized.

What is "voice" in fiction? Hoeper and Pickering (1982) explain what the writer does to evoke his or her authorial voice or invent a character's voice:

> From early childhood on we learn to identify and respond to these elements of speech (accent, inflection, and duration) in a speaker's voice. For example, a mother can tell her child to "Come here!" in a manner that is angry, threatening, concerned, amused, sympathetic, or affectionate simply by altering her tone of voice. In each case, the mother's *meaning* is the same--she wants her child to come. However, the relationship she creates with her auditor (the child) will differ dramatically according to her tone. . . . The particular qualities of a speaking voice are unavailable to a writer in creating tone, but to a certain extent rhythm and punctuation can substitute for a speaker's accent and inflection, while word order and word choice can influence tone as easily in prose as in speech. (p. 64)

While such voices do not belong to authentic human speakers, they represent the most authentic collection of voices available apart from actual human speech. Often they have even more variety and more vitality than actual speech. Students certainly cannot hope to visit enough cities, towns, and suburbs or meet enough people to hear a complete cross-section of voices speaking English. However, fiction offers a modest substitute for such opportunities and provides models from which students can develop a voice in English.

How does the student gain access to this array of voices? Of course, the student interested in tuning in to fictional voices can simply read, aloud preferably, sections of short stories and hear, for example, the situation of a doctor in William Carlos Williams' "The Use of Force" or of an arguing huband and wife in Katherine Anne Porter's "Rope." Henderson (1983) suggests that the ironic voice may be taught in a direct fashion by having students underline the words and phrases they hear as irony and discuss the properties of these words that make them ironic. Asking the student to tell the story from another point of view will help reveal the essence of the irony through different perspectives. Assigning students to collect examples on cassette of distinct voices they hear in supermarkets, on television, and on radio--voices that approach the voices they have heard in the stories, can sharpen their awareness of voice. Drawing a face associated with a fictional voice can encourage students to notice tone more fully. The most interesting and significant way in which short fiction can be made accessible to second language learners may be the activities that ingenious students and teachers devise themselves.

As students read, learn about, and enjoy short stories, literary interpretation of the story begins, often unintentionally. If it does not occur consciously, it may get under way as the result of a question or remark about the tale. Literary interpretation may take place under various guises, such as thematic discussion, literary understanding, and so on. In all of these, the students study the story not to improve their grammar or to develop a distinctive voice in English, or for any other functional purpose, but to interpret it as literature.

What kind of activities will such study involve? This question may concern a single aspect of the story or the entire story. Costa (1983) selects an appropriate area of a short story for study. Topics include conflict, irony, endings, point of view, and others. McConochie (1975) applies this typical approach through comprehension and discussion questions. Mullen (1984) leads the reader to understand each component of the story and then exhorts him or her to probe for deeper meaning. Thus the activities of literary interpretation, far from being esoteric, are simply questions about the story's significance and directions to students to search for such meanings. When the questions are well thought out and both imaginatively and pleasantly put forth, the technique is effective. But requests to search for aspects that the instructor considers profound and that are not tied to the students' experience of the story cannot hold their attention.

What literary interpretation can and should be if it is undertaken in the ESL context is a system of questions and directions that stimulate discussion, both about the literature and about the culture in which it is set. Povey (1984) says his anthology "provides a unique method of challenging their linguistic handicaps through productive and original classroom activities, both oral and written. It introduces topics appropriate to their sophistication and learning--presenting American beliefs and behavior through literature to stimulate and sustain vigorous intercultural discussion" (p. v). He includes (a) essential and well-structured background material for each story; (b) the stories with minimal glosses; and (c) end material, including basic comprehension questions, questions to ponder concerning the characters and plot, questions to lead students to consider the major issues of the stories, and ideas for discussion. As Leki (1984) has rightly observed, "Although Povey does not introduce the traditional apparatus for literary analysis (for example, characterization, plot, theme, the elements of fiction) his detailed and thoughtful summaries and culture notes are perhaps more immediately useful as introduction to the stories" (pp. 732-33). Activities at this level are neither bald questions about meaning nor exhortations to students to look for something deep. Instead, activities are the best, the most interesting and most catalytic questions students can be asked to consider and discuss. The net effect of these questions is that they get students thinking about and questioning the assumptions of the culture in which they are currently living, the culture from which they came, and their identities in both.

Of course even advanced students may find it difficult at times, even with such questions a guides, to muster enough language resources or to integrate them sufficiently to ask questions about the society in which they reside and whose language they are learning. If so, simpler activities can usually aid the student to become immersed in, understand, and question cultural assumptions in the target language; to cross, in Marshall's (1979) words, "those barriers of time and culture across which all literature functions" (p. 332). Role playing particular culture-based points of view, for example, is a time-honored, useful activity. It helps the students to recognize models of individuals within the target culture. Again, modifying the ending of a story in terms of the student's native culture can sharpen his or her perception of cultural differences, as can changing words to reflect cultural differences. Debate is a useful follow-up to a story that opens one or another cultural value or assumption to new scrutiny. While these and other similar activities are not unique to literature-based classes, they take on a special richness in this context.

Fiction lends itself to a special brand of ESL activity. The activity it stimulates is not perceived as a series of tasks, but received with an excitement and a joy derived from the thought and feeling that readers are moved to bring to that life. In contrast, some texts blandly apply a rigid formula and format for exposing the ESL reader to fiction. It can be hoped that this unoriginal approach has little future.

The movement back to the story itself should be encouraged, drawing on the magic of storytelling, listening, and responding or reacting to the tale. This old tradition, applied to the ESL context, needs few if any devices or activities. Activity arises from the story's inherent power to engender discussion and debate to get students involved. Such involvement is guaranteed when reader/listeners are caught by a good story's revelation of the self or a persona in a culture. Common sense says that understanding and then expressing feelings are among the most interesting and healthiest processes available to human beings. Indeed, this is what it means to become an interpreter of literature.

5
The Place of Literature in the Teaching of ESL

Marckwardt (1978) states some general principles about how literature can best be used in ESL contexts. Because of the flexible nature of literature, the role of literature in the ESL curriculum varies according to the specific situation and the aims of teaching English. This is the natural starting point for determining the best use of literature in the curriculum. Many diverse suggestions are naturally to be expected. The most frequently stated purposes include (a) appreciation and enjoyment of literature; (b) the refinement of language skills; (c) the stimulation of more advanced learning; (d) a stimulus for advanced discussion; and (e) personal growth.

The primary purpose of literature in ESL--that of appreciation and enjoyment--does not conflict with the goal of learning (Povey, 1967). Indeed, the promise of enjoyment is a key to making learning desirable. Literature can also, according to O'Brien and Young (1979), help "students consolidate previously learned but not necessarily well-acquired skills" (p. 582), putting the finishing touches on the students' language development. Another optimum use of fiction, poetry, and drama is, according to Bradford (1968), to stimulate further and more advanced study.

In short, literature must challenge students to attain more and more knowledge and develop their cognitive abilities. To this end, the teacher should not select literature that is too elementary. While the reader must understand what words mean,

> if the reader understands the language of a story, then the story will be of no value to him as a language learning device. . . . Similarly, a story can teach sentence structure only if that story introduces sentence structures with which the reader is not familiar. (Bradford, 1968, p. 205)

It is not strictly accurate that students learn only when they are exposed to unfamiliar structures, as it has been shown that prior knowledge contributes to learning. Nevertheless Bradford makes an important point: Literature is used well when it is used to challenge and prod students to learn more. He also urges that literature be used in ESL only if it teaches more effectively than other prose forms. This criterion may be overly restrictive. However, the point remains that literature is put to optimum use when it stimulates the reader's learning. According to Widdowson (1975): "The reader of literature has his expectations aroused by the patterns of language which give shape to the writer's perceptions of this other reality and then experiences its elusiveness as these expectations are denied when the patterns change" (p. 70). The reader, then, is stimulated to discover how the unique patterns of literary language develop.

A final optimum use of literature concerns the reader himself or herself. Literature can and should stimulate the person's overall growth. It should be a starting point for higher-level discussions concerning the self in all its aspects and especially within the target culture. It offers the reader an opportunity for catharsis and the integration of discordant and conflicting forces in his or her life. If successfully absorbed, literature stimulates growth. As McKay (1982) explains, the reading of literature can be an intense personal experience. It can stimulate personal, moral, psychological, emotional, and intellectual growth. It should develop what DiPietro (1982) says ESL teachers have neglected, "a concept of the learner as a whole person " (p. 215).

How much English do students need to begin to discover and take advantage of these benefits? Opinions abound concerning the prerequisites for beginning to work with a poem, a story, or a play. McConochie (1979) expresses a definite point of view in her article demonstrating the use of poetry for young learners. She recommends beginning teaching children poetry when they are between the ages of 5 and 10. Allen (1979) generally concurs, advocating poetry and stories for children even at age 3, and she too offers specific suggestions. Adults also need, like, and can learn from literature, and DiPietro (1983) says not enough has been done for this group with literature, leaving "largely unaddressed the question of what to do at higher levels where the reading of literature has been undertaken" (p. 44). This tendency is changing rapidly but remains an issue. The question of what linguistic level is most appropriate for beginning teaching literature to ESL students persists for many (Muyskens, 1983):

> [One scholar] suggests that literary texts be introduced at beginning levels in order to prepare students to approach

literature effectively in college. Not all foreign language educators agree, however. Esler and Bolinger, for example, strongly urge that students be well prepared linguistically before entering into the intricacies of literature. This debate on the separation between language and literary study is not new. Castaneda, for one, firmly believes that language can and indeed should be taught through literature. (p. 413)

Muyskens' criterion for deciding when it is best to introduce literature into foreign language learning centers on the learner.

Whether literature is introduced early or late in a student's ESL training, another question arises: How should the literature most effectively be used? Some of the many models, suggestions, and possibilities have been described here. Ashmead (1965) offers additional ways to treat target language literary materials in an ESL context. Such models stimulate the ingenuity of other ESL professionals to develop additional opportunities for students and teachers to enjoy literature. Marckwardt (1978) discusses obstacles such as the traditional way of teaching the native literature in a particular place. But such real limitations may be overcome in the process of creating the widest variety of study opportunities for ESL students that literature surely allows.

When and how often should literature be used in ESL? That is, how much literature should be included in the ESL curriculum? There are no definite answers or certain rules. Widdowson (1983) points out that no one urges the exclusive use of literature in ESL. But like communicative syllabi, the Silent Way, Total Physical Response, and the myriad other language methods on the market, literature is "an available resource" (p. 34). It is a valuable resource with many optimum uses for teachers and students.

6
Guidelines for Selecting and Editing Literature for the ESL Classroom

No discussion of literature and ESL is complete without guidelines for selecting and preparing literary materials for classroom use by ESL teachers and students. In fact, both stages are crucial to the enjoyment and study of literature. Unless both stages are handled well, literature study will not be fruitful or last very long in the ESL world. In addition, the preparation of teachers is crucial to the learning of literature in an ESL context. These two matters have been so thoroughly discussed elsewhere that only the rough lines of the various alternatives are sketched here.

In general, the barriers between the literature and the student should be kept to a minimum. Sometimes a barrier is a linguistic item that is too difficult for the student (e.g., unfamiliar vocabulary). But sometimes barriers are created through devices that editors may think help students but actually confuse them. Simplified, abridged, and glossed texts abound in the ESL publishing world, despite the dangers of textual distortion inherent in such alterations. They are rarely uniform, and rarely adhere to their purpose. A recent view of simplified literary texts is offered by Mitchell (1984). Marckwardt (1978) points out that some "simplified texts change constructions and words and often make the original length longer" (p. 54). Such editions concentrate on vocabulary simplification, but are not concerned about complex syntax, which is an equally important aspect of any text. Abridgements or reductions often greatly distort texts, and for this reason are strenuously avoided.

How useful are adaptations? Marckwardt (1978) concludes through an analysis of a Jack London abridgement that each alteration represents gains and losses that must be weighed carefully. Others are more vehemently committed to one or another position about altered texts. O'Brien and Young (1979) declare that advanced students want to and can handle unedited texts. Bradford (1968) urges the use of complete pieces but acknowledges that excerpts are sometimes necessary and should be treated as complete units. Ashmead (1967) considers abridgements to be downright destructive: "I do not regard the attempt of one series to reduce *Moby-Dick* to 2400 words, *Huck Finn* to 2400 words, or *Portrait of a Lady* to 2000 words, as aids in the teaching of the American novel--quite the reverse" (p. 15). Slager (1965), in a discussion of the problems of selecting and editing literature for ESL, states, "An introduction to imaginative literature should not present simplified versions" because they "have no place in a literature anthology" (p. 129). He did, however, shorten some selections without, he feels, destroying the pieces. Muyskens (1983) seems to agree with Slager but notes the difficulty of finding unabridged works with sufficient introductory and supporting materials.

The opposite position is represented as much by those who discuss their actual classroom practices of using simplified texts (e.g., Abercrombie, 1963), assuming such texts are necessary, as by those who formally suggest that not enough is known about foreign students' readiness for unaltered texts. Arguments for altered texts often point out student unreadiness rather than directly suggesting text modification. They often also show up in arguments for the selection of literature, as discussed later in this section.

The amount of direct contact with an unaltered literature text that is appropriate for ESL students depends first of all on their level in English: beginning, intermediate, or advanced. Two crucial linguistic factors are vocabulary and syntax. Marckwardt (1978) says the importance of the vocabulary problem is probably overstated. Acknowledging that students may encounter many unfamiliar words in a single piece of literature, he favors vocabulary acquisition through context and repeated contact, rather than through memorization. He suggests also that students study prefixes, suffices, and cognates, and use an English-only dictionary. Slager (1965) concurs, with the reminder that even though the dictionary helps only with conventional senses of words, it is an important but not exclusive source of linguistic information.

The situation with syntax is not as clear primarily because of a lack of knowledge about its real complexity for ESL students. Scott (1964) states, "We've no readily available tabulation of syntactic structures in terms of their frequency of occurrence, as we do for vocabulary items" (p. 492), and points out the need for a more scientific approach to syntax. Harris and Harris (1967) also discuss the lack of verifiable syntactic information. Thus scholars and teachers may have a sense of the extent of lexical and syntactical

Guidelines for Selecting and Editing 75

difficulties of literature for ESL students, but they have no empirical measure of difficulty.

A related question is whether determining the precise difficulty of words and sentences for ESL students is pertinent to their success. Can they learn from unedited literature without their teachers--or they themselves, for that matter--knowing which words and sentences they find most difficult? Potter (1983) explains that readers absorb the meaning of a text according to general and specific background information that they bring to the task. Scholars generally concur that students need not comprehend everything they read, as general comprehension occurs despite the inability to grasp various difficult structures (Buckton, 1983; Povey, 1967). Indeed, Barry (1983) argues that an overload of linguistic information can hurt rather than help fluency.

The most difficult challenge of literature is lessened by cultural knowledge. ESL professionals agree that when cultural information is incorporated in the text students grasp complex material more readily. Povey (1967) suggests that cultural barriers are more likely than language difficulties to confuse students. Thus the selection and preparation of literature for students must take culture into account and help students understand it. In discussing Matthew Arnold's "The Scholar Gypsy," for example, Munro (1969) acknowledges that students who are intimidated by the poem cannot appreciate it. However, he does not believe glossings are a solution. Marshall (1979) gives the example of attempting to teach Hopkins' "Spring and Fall" in a tropical climate where snow simply is not among the elements. This barrier is indeed a challenge. Text material should be replete with cultural information and edited to help students recreate the scene they are reading about, perhaps even visually (Buckton, 1983). In such a situation the book functions as a prop, offering the kind of cultural orientation, for example, that helped Laygo's (1978) Filipino students appreciate and effectively interpret two American short stories. Thus literature that strikes "a balance between writing which stresses cultural universality, and the generality of human emotions, and those cultural elements which are most specifically and individually American" (Povey, 1967, p. 44) is most accessible for ESL students. Even though true biculturality may be impossible, it may be a reasonable educational goal (Marckwardt, 1978).

In addition to the obligation to supply nonnative students with essential cultural information, the editors of literary ESL texts need to meet several criteria. These criteria include (a) contemporaneity, (b) cultural and geographical inclusiveness, (c) brevity,

(d) accessibility of style and appropriateness to the students' level, (e) completeness, and (f) cultural significance and interest, or universality.

Editor's Criteria

Contemporaneity. Few scholars or critics find fault with the criterion of contemporaneity. Old words and distant historical events add little to ESL students' experience of literature, and may even discourage them. When students can see in the literature aspects of the target culture they encounter in daily life, they receive a learning reinforcement (Adeyanju, 1978).

Inclusiveness. The literature chosen should represent as much of the English-speaking world as possible (Marckwardt, 1978). Slager (1965) notes that such literature is easily accessible--literature from Nigeria, India, Ireland, and so on.

Brevity. The works should be relatively brief. Except for novels, discussed shortly, brevity will improve the teacher's chances of maintaining students' interest throughout a lesson. If they have to struggle for too long with an unfamiliar text, they may lose interest (Adeyanju, 1978).

Accessibility of Style. The work should have an accessible style (Adeyanju, 1978). Indeed, style is a major factor in determining whether the piece is literary (Slager, 1965). The works should have interest value for ESL students; fiction's plots and subject matter should be attractive (Adeyanju, 1978).

Completeness. As discussed, many teachers feel complete works are best, if only, as Marckwardt (1978) suggests, "to demonstrate that literary works do have a beginning, a middle, and an end" (p. 67).

Cultural Significance. Finally, they should be culturally significant and, if possible, universal (Adeyanju, 1978). Interestingly, several scholars agree that a work need not be a classic or great literature to be useful in ESL (Povey, 1979; Widdowson, 1975). At the same time, notes Slager (1965), "writers of distinction" are "just as accessible as writers of lesser stature" (p. 129), if chosen carefully. He contends that Faulkner, James, and Conrad have prohibitively complex styles. But such a blanket exclusion of

Guidelines for Selecting and Editing 77

authors is unwarranted once teachers know how to select and present literary works for ESL.

Beyond these criteria, generally speaking, the literature chosen should consider and be related to the surrounding society and its learning goals. In most cultures, literature is a way to preserve and transmit the cultural heritage (Marckwardt, 1978). Observation of local education and the state of English provides a starting point from which to develop a nonnative literary curriculum.

Briefly presented, these are the main criteria used repeatedly in the selection of literature for ESL students. Jacoby (1985) and Leki (1984) provide comprehensive surveys of two contemporary anthologies aimed at ESL students. But what literature are these students actually reading outside of class? They are reading mysteries with short but complex plots and clear solutions (Heringer, 1979), and other crime narratives, attracted by their motivational value (Kerschgens, 1978). Several teachers and scholars have recorded their ESL students' experiences with contemporary and recent writers (Hergt, 1978; Hoegel, 1977; Marckwardt, 1978; Meltzer, 1984; Scherwionke, 1978; Wolter, 1977). DiPietro (1982) stresses the importance of using ethnic themes and writers in ESL classes, suggesting particular pieces and authors. This approach is simply another dimension of the need for inclusiveness regarding the literatures available in English to ESL teachers and students. The literature of the world is "a single broad panorama" (Marckwardt, 1978, p. 29), replete with valuable literary resources. The vast body includes traditional classics, modern innovations, and perennial children's favorites (Marckwardt, 1978); stories that need acting out and nonverbal clues (Bradford, 1968); and possibilities beyond any one teacher's imagining.

The potential of the novel in the ESL classroom has been, to some extent, a separate question, primarily because of its length. While the other selection criteria easily apply to the novel, the issue of length is a unique criterion with respect to the novel. It involves the question of how to maintain students' interest throughout a long, perhaps complex story. Another question is how to obtain what are, in some instances, not easily available materials. Fortunately, solutions are available, ranging from Marckwardt's (1978) suggestion to select chapters or episodes to be read in English while the remainder of the novel is read in translation to Yorke's (1980) procedure: clip key passages from the first two-thirds of a novel; give one passage to each student; have students read and prepare their excerpts for presentation to the class; finally, the entire class can read the final third of the novel. Such suggestions seek to avoid the dreary reading of long, culturally distant novels that nonnative readers find distasteful (Kumar, 1978). As noted earlier, connotation and abridgement may not solve this problem. Innovative use of authentic materials, such as those described, if well-arranged, can play a valid role in ESL while the full work remains easily available nearby.

In this regard, more, not less, than the full work is necessary. Slager (1965) has pointed out how introductory materials, well-chosen biographical facts, and explanations, when appropriate, can aid (not interfere with) comprehension. One example is the need to explain to some students what the Oedipus complex is before they read Frank O'Conner's "My Oedipus Complex." In addition, short supplementary manuals can enable readers to find information if and when they require it.

The best and most important resource--by no means supplementary--is the teacher. The best selected and edited literary materials are simply not sufficient without teachers. The most serious lack in ESL instruction is not that of appropriate literary materials but that of teachers trained well enough to use them as they become available. Widdowson (1983) observes:

> As language teaching increasingly chose linguistics as its point of reference, literature was ruled out of court very largely because linguists, generally speaking, are not literary scholars. It's amazing how much philistinism there is among linguists and applied linguists. It's rather surprising how few people concerned with language these days have any interest in or knowledge about literature. (p. 34)

The absence of methodology courses in teaching literature has been cited as a current deficiency in the curriculum (Muyskens, 1983).

Perhaps the key word in learning about using literature in ESL is not training, with its rigid connotations, but exposure. Nevertheless, the real work of making literature accessible and enjoyable to ESL students and teachers lies not in materials selection, but in the best teacher-training and in-service courses possible. Sensitivity exercises and sessions can help teachers who are intimidated by literature to become more aware that it is an already-familiar use of the language. On a larger scale, graduate seminars can be offered on literature and ESL. Such education can take many forms, as administrators, scholars, and teachers seek to address their needs. Whatever resources they invent or discover, teachers will ultimately feel freer to make full use of, enjoy, and even create original literary materials for their students' use and appreciation.

References/Resources

References

Abercrombie, D. (1963). Conversation and spoken prose. *English Language Teaching, 18*, 10-16.

Adeyanju, T.K. (1978). Teaching literature and human values in ESL: Objectives and selection. *English Language Teaching Journal, 32*, 133-138.

Allen, V.F. (1978). Some insights from linguistics for the teaching of literature. In M.K. Burt & H. Dulay (Eds.), *New directions in second language learning* (pp. 319-327). Washington, DC: Teachers of English to Speakers of Other Languages.

Allen, V.G. (1979). Books to lead the non-English speaking student into literature. *Reading Teacher, 32*, 940-946.

Arnold, M. (1963). *The poetical works of Matthew Arnold.* Lowry, H.F. & Tinker, G.B. (Eds.). London: Oxford University Press.

Ashmead, J. (1965). Whitman's "Wintry Locomotive," export model. In V.F. Allen (Ed.), *On teaching English to speakers of other languages: Papers read at the TESOL conference, May 8-9, 1964, Tucson, AZ* (pp. 154-158). Champaign, IL: National Council of Teachers of English.

Ashmead, J. (1967). Innocents abroad--Teaching the American novel overseas. *TESOL Quarterly, 1*(3), 11-16.

Balakian, A. (1977). Teaching language and literature. *Teaching Language Through Literature, 16*, 1-5.

Barnet, S., Berman, M., & Burto, W. (Eds.). (1967). *An introduction to literature* (3rd ed.). Boston: Little, Brown.

Barry, P. (1983). Discourse analysis revisited: A reply to H. Sopher and Tony Deyes. *ELT Journal, 37*, 44-47.

Blatchford, C.H. (1972). ESOL and literature: A negative view. *Culture and Language Learning Newsletter, 1*, 6-7.

Blatchford, C.H. (1974). Should literature be a part of TESOL? *English Teaching Forum, 12*, 46-49.

Bolinger, D. (1968). Literature yes, but when? *Hispania, 51*, 118-119.

Bradford, A. (1968). Reading literature and learning a second language. *Language Learning, 18*, 199-210.

Branden, N. (1980). *The psychology of romantic love.* New York: Bantam Books.

Brod, E.F. (1983). A linguistic technique for the foreign language classroom. *Foreign Language Annals, 16*, 255-271.

Brooks, C., & Warren, R.P. (1960). *Understanding poetry.* New York: Holt, Rinehart, and Winston.

Buckton, R.J. (1983). An approach to Western literature for Arab students. *British Journal of Language Teaching, 21*, 86-92.

Charlesworth, R.A. (1978). The role of literature in the teaching of English as a second dialect. *English Quarterly, 11*, 157-177.

Charters, A. (Ed.). (1983). *The story and its writer: An introduction to short fiction.* New York: St. Martin's Press.

Christison, M.A. (1982). *English through poetry.* San Francisco: Alemany Press.

Christison, M.A. (1982). Using poetry in ESL. *TESOL Newsletter, 16*, 9.

Costa, G. (1983). *American short stories: Exercises in reading and writing.* New York: Harcourt, Brace, Jovanovich.

Crane, S. (1955). "The Open Boat." In R.W. Stallman (Ed.), *Stephen Crane: Stories and tales* (pp. 215-237). New York: Random House.

Crane, S. (1981). "A Man Said to the Universe." In S. Bradley, E.H. Long, & G. Perkins (Eds.), *The American tradition in literature* (5th ed.) (p. 1241). New York: Random House.

Current-Garcia, E., & Patrick, W. (1961). *What is the short story?* Chicago: Scott Foresman.

DiPietro, R.J. (1982). The multi-ethnicity of American literature: A neglected resource for the EFL teacher. In M. Hines & W.

Rutherford (Eds.). *On TESOL '81* (pp. 215-229). Washington, DC: Teachers of English to Speakers of Other Languages. (ERIC Document Reproduction Service No. ED 223 097)

DiPietro, R.J. (1983). Interaction with texts in the ESL/EFL classroom. *Canadian Modern Language Review, 40,* 44-50.

Emmanuel, J. (1983). *A poet's mind.* New York: Regents.

Esler, R.C. (1968). The teaching of literature to whom. *Hispania, 51,* 847-848.

Gatbonton, E., & Tucker, G.R. (1971). Cultural orientation and the study of literature. *TESOL Quarterly, 5,* 137-143.

Gibson, R.E. (1975). The strip story: A catalyst for communication. *TESOL Quarterly, 9,* 149-152.

Harris, A.S., & Harris, A.S. (1967). A selected bibliography of American literature for TESOL. *TESOL Quarterly, 1,* 53-62.

Hayden, R. (1975). *Angle of ascent: New and selected poems.* New York: Liveright.

Hemingway, E. (1970). *The Nick Adams Stories.* New York: Scribner.

Henderson, D. (1983). Teaching the short story to ESL students entering college. *TESOL Newsletter, 17,* 13-14.

Hergt, T. (1978). Vom Gehilfen zum Helfer: Das Thema der Mitmenschlichkeit in Bernard Malamud's "The Assistant" [From assistant to helper: The theme of mutual helpfulness in Bernard Malamud's "The Assistant."] *Neusprachliche Mitteilungen, 31,* 74-81.

Heringer, V. (1979). A whodunit in the ESL classroom. *English Language Teaching Journal, 34,* 37-39.

Hilferty, A., & Lezberg, A. (1979). Discourse analysis in the reading class. *TESOL Quarterly, 12,* 47-55.

Hoejel, R. (1977). Today is Friday: A religious dramatic scene from E. Hemingway in English teaching. *Praxis des neusprachlichen Unterrichts, 24,* 41-46.

Hoeper, J.D., & Pickering, J.H. (1982). *Literature.* New York: Macmillan.

Jacoby, S. (1985). Outsiders: American short stories for students of ESL. *TESOL Newsletter, 19,* 17, 19.

Keats, J. (1959). "On the Grasshopper and the Cricket." In D. Bush (Ed.), *Selected poems and letters* (p. 19). Boston: Houghton Mifflin.

Kerschgens, E. (1978). Who killed Baker: A crime story in the Hauptschule. *English, 13*, 50-54.

Kintanar, T. (1972). The role of literature in culture learning. *Culture and Language Learning Newsletter, 1*, 1-5.

Kolb, M. (1983). An analysis of Robert Hayden's "Those Winter Sundays." Unpublished manuscript.

Kujoory, P. (1978). Iranian students and western cultural concepts in literature. *English Language Teaching Journal, 32*, 221-225.

Kumar, S. (1978). Introducing classics to undergraduates. *English Language Teaching Journal, 4*, 301-303.

Kuntz, L. Poetry at PASS. *Passage 2*(2), 53-55.

Lardner, R. (1981). "Haircut." In R.V. Cassell (Ed.), *The Norton anthology of short fiction* (pp. 786-795). New York: W.W. Norton.

Laygo, T. (1978). *The well of time: Teacher's handbook*. Berkeley, CA: Asian-American Bilingual Center. (ERIC Document Reproduction Service No. ED 189 827)

Lezberg, A., & Hilferty, A. (1978). Discourse analysis in the reading class. *TESOL Quarterly, 12*, 47-55.

Lee, W.R. (1970). Editorial. *English Language Teaching, 25*, 1-2.

Leki, R. (1984). Review of *Outsiders: American short stories for students of ESL and literature for discussion: A reader for advanced students of English as a second language. TESOL Quarterly, 18*, 729-735.

MacLeish, A. (1982). "Ars poetica." In L. Perrine (Ed.), *Sound and sense* (6th ed.) (p. 136). New York: Harcourt, Brace, Jovanovich.

Maher, J.C. (1981). Graded poetry composition. *English Language Teaching Journal, 35*, 168-171.

Marckwardt, A.H. (1978). *The place of literature in the teaching of English as a second or foreign language*. Honolulu: East-West Center. (ERIC Document Reproduction Service No. ED 168 360)

Marckwardt, A.H. (1981). What literature to teach: Principles of selection and class treatment. *English Teaching Forum, 19*, 2-7.

Marquardt, W.F. (1968). Literature and cross cultural communication. *English Teaching Forum, 6,* 8-10.

Marshall, M. (1979). Love and death in Eden: Teaching English literature to ESL students. *TESOL Quarterly, 13,* 331-338.

McConochie, J.A. (1975). *Twentieth century American short stories.* New York: Collier Macmillan.

McConochie, J.A. (1979). "Cottleston, Cottleston, Cottleston Pie". Poetry and verse for young learners. *English Teaching Forum, 17,* 6-12.

McConochie, J.A. (1982). All this fiddle: Enhancing language awareness through poetry. In M. Hines & W. Rutherford (Eds.), *On TESOL '81* (pp. 231-240). Washington, DC: Teachers of English to Speakers of Other Languages. (ERIC Document Reproduction Service No. ED 223 098)

McConochie, J.A. (1985). Musing on the lamp flame: Teaching a narrative poem in a college-level ESOL class. *TESOL Quarterly, 19,* 125-136.

McConochie, J.A., & Sage, H. (1985). Since feeling is first: Thoughts on sharing poetry in the ESOL classroom. *English Teaching Forum, 23,* 2-5.

McKay, S. (1980). Review of Louise M. Rosenblatt's *The reader, the text, the poem; The transactional theory of the literary work. TESOL Quarterly, 14,* 379-381.

McKay, S. (1982). Literature in the ESL classroom. *TESOL Quarterly, 16,* 529-536.

Meltzer, H.M. (1977). "Anti-Utopia" in language teaching: A pedagogical perspective from the example of Orwell's *1984. Neusprachliche Mitteilungen, 30,* 153-158.

Mitchell, B. (1984). Unpublished master's thesis, University of California at Los Angeles.

Moody, H.L.B. (1971). *The teaching of literature in developing countries.* London: Longman Group.

Mullen, J. (1984). *Outsiders: American short stories for students of ESL.* Englewood Cliffs, NJ: Prentice-Hall.

Munro, J.M. (1969). Teaching English as a foreign language. *The Educational Forum, 3,* 321-328.

Muyskens, J.A. (1983). Teaching second-language literatures: Past, present, and future. *The Modern Language Journal, 67*, 413-423.

Nowottny, W. (1965). *The language poets use*. London: Athlone Press.

O'Brien, T., & Young, L. (1979). English for academic purposes through Canadian literature and history. *Canadian Modern Language Review, 35*, 581-587.

Oller, J.W. (1983). Story writing principles and ESL teaching. *TESOL Quarterly, 17*, 39-53.

Perrine, L. (1982). *Sound and sense: An introduction to poetry* (6th ed.). New York: Harcourt, Brace, Jovanovich.

Pincas, A. (1963). Cultural translation for foreign students of English language and literature. *Language Learning, 3*, 15-26.

Potter, J. (1983). Reading for pleasure with an intermediate level of English. *MEXTESOL Journal, 7*, 9-21 (ERIC Document Reproduction Service No. ED 240 873)

Povey, J.F. (1967). Literature in TESL programs: The language and the culture. *TESOL Quarterly, 1, 40-46*.

Povey, J.F. Poetry in the ESL class. In M.R. Bracy (Ed.), *Working Papers in English as a Second Language* III (pp. 25-30). Los Angeles: University of California.

Povey, J.F (1979). The teaching of literature in advanced ESL classes. In L. McIntosh & M. Celce-Murcia (Eds.), *Teaching English as a second or foreign language* (pp. 162-186). Rowley, MA: Newbury House.

Povey, J. (1984). *Literature for discussion*. New York: Holt, Rinehart, and Winston.

Povey, J. (1986). Using literature with ESL students. *ERIC/CLL News Bulletin, 10*(1), 3-4.

Preston, W. (1982). Poetry ideas in teaching literature and writing to foreign students. *TESOL Quarterly, 16*, 489-502.

Randall, D. (1981). "Ballad of Birmingham." In J.P. Hunter (Ed.), *The Norton introduction to poetry* (p. 74). New York: W.W. Norton.

Reese, A.L. (1979). Serial story reading in class. *English Language Teaching Journal, 33*, 301-303.

Rosenblatt, L.M. (1978). *The reader, the text, the poem: The transactional theory of the literary work*. Carbondale, IL: Southern Illinois University Press.

Sage, H. (1983). Review of *A Poet's Mind*. TESOL Newsletter, 17, 15, 17.

Sage, H. (1983, March). Short, sweet, and sticky: Short fiction for ESOL instruction. Paper presented at the Annual Convention of Teachers of English to Speakers of Other Languages, March 15-20, 1983, Toronto, Canada. (ERIC Document Reproduction Service No. 234 610)

Santoni, G. (1983). Letter to Judith A. Muyskens. In J.A. Muyskens, Teaching second language literatures: Past, present, and future. *The Modern Language Journal, 67*, 413-423.

Scherwionke, M. (1978). Poetic documentation of an historical event--The Dublin Easter uprising of 1916· Design for a 5-hour weekly course in English. *Neusprachliche Mitteilungen, 31*, 15-20.

Schlepper, W. (1979). Zur Wortschatzarbeit auf der Sekundarstufe. [Vocabulary work in grades 11-13]. *Neusprachliche Mitteilungen, 32*, 177-183.

Schneider, R. (1977). Sherlock Holmes in English literature at the lower secondary level. *Praxis des Neusprachlichen Unterrichts, 24*, 359-370.

Scott, C.T. (1964). Literature and the ESL program. *The Modern Language Journal, 48*, 489-493.

Slager, W.R. (1965). Introducing *Literature in English:* Problems in selecting and editing. In V.F. Allen (Ed.), (pp. 128-132). *On teaching English to speakers of other languages: Papers read at the TESOL conference*, Tucson, Arizona, May 8-9, 1964. Champaign, IL: National Council of Teachers of English.

Spinelli, E., & Williams, S.A. (1981). From language to literature: Figurative language in the college foreign language class. *Foreign Language Annals, 14*, 37-43.

Spuler, R. (1981). Concrete poetry and elementary language study. *Teaching Language Through Literature, 20*, 36-37.

Stevens, W. (1957). "The Man Whose Pharynx Was Bad." In S.F. Morse (Ed.), *Poems by Wallace Stevens* (p. 22). New York: Random House.

Topping, D.M. (1968). Linguistics or literature. *TESOL Quarterly*, 2, 95-100.

Tuers, E. (1971). A cultural approach to the teaching of reading in ESL. In *Proceedings of Seminar on Teaching of English Language in Iran*, (pp. 18-25). Tehran, Iran: Department of University Relations and Cooperation.

Waldinger, A. (1980). Retelling: Composition for young learners from Russia. *Language Arts*, 57, 52-55.

Watts, M. (1981). Writing poetry and learning English. *English Language Teaching Journal*, 35, 444-450.

Welty, E. (1966). "Powerhouse." In J. Moffett & K. McElhany (Eds.), *Points of view* (pp. 523-535). New York: New American Library.

White, R. (1977). Telling what happened. *TESOL Quarterly*, 11, 271-281.

Whitman, W. (1958). "Song of Myself." In G.W. Allen (Ed.), *Leaves of grass* (pp. 49-96). New York: New American Library.

Widdowson, H. (1975). *Stylistics and the teaching of literature*. London: Longman.

Widdowson, H. (1982). The use of literature. In M. Hines & W. Rutherford (Eds.), *On TESOL '81* (pp. 203-214). Washington, DC: Teachers of English to Speakers of Other Languages.

Widdowson, H. (1983). Talking shop: On literature and ELT. *ELT Journal*, 37, 30-35.

Williams, W.C. (1975). The use of force. In J.A. McConochie (Ed.), *20th century American short stories* (pp. 8-11). New York: Collier Macmillan.

Wolf, D. (1984). Research currents about language skills from narration. *Language Arts*. 61, 844-850.

Wolfe, T. (1957). *Look homeward, angel*. New York: Scribners.

Wolfe, T. (1962). "Only the Dead Know Brooklyn." In C. Hugh Holman (Ed.), *The Thomas Wolfe reader* (pp. 465-469). New York: Scribners.

Wolfson, N. (1979). A feature of performed narrative: The conversational historical present. *Language in Society*, 7, 215-237.

Wolter, J. (1977). O'Neill's short drama "Fog" in English teaching. *Praxis des Neusprachlichen Unterrichts, 24*, 3.

Yorke, M. (1980). Encountering the novel: Problems and a possible solution. *English Language Teaching Journal, 34*, 215-237.

Resources

Poetry Anthologies and Guides

Adoff, A. (Ed.). (1968). *I am the darker brother: An anthology of modern poems by black Americans.* New York: Macmillan.

Bass, E., & Howe, H. (Eds.). (1973). *No more masks: An anthology of poems by women.* New York: Doubleday.

Bontemps, A. (Ed.). (1963). *American Negro poetry.* New York: Hill and Wang.

Deutsch, B. (1974). *Poetry handbook.* New York: Funk and Wagnals.

Ellman, R. (Ed.). (1976). *The new Oxford book of American verse.* New York: Oxford University Press.

Hibbard, A., Holman, C.H., & Thrall, W.F. (Eds.). (1960). *A handbook to literature.* New York: Odyssey Press.

Smith, A.J. (Ed.). (1967). *Seven centuries of verse.* New York: Scribner's.

Fiction Anthologies and Guides

Cassill, R.V. (Ed.). (1978). *The Norton anthology of short fiction.* New York: W.W. Norton.

Clayton, J.J. (Ed.). (1977). *The Heath introduction to fiction.* Boston: D.C. Heath.

Frakes, J.R., & Isadore Traschen, I. (Eds.) (1959). *Short fiction: A critical collection.* Englewood Cliffs, NJ: Prentice-Hall.

Issacs, N.D., & Leiter, L.H. (Eds.). (1963). *Approaches to the short story.* San Francisco: Chandler.

McConochie, J.A. (Ed.). (1975). *20th century American short stories.* New York: Collier Macmilan.

Newman, K.D. (Ed.). (1975). *Ethnic American short stories.* New York: Washington Square Press.

Perrine, L. (Ed.). (1974). *Story and structure.* New York: Harcourt, Brace Jovanovich.

Sources of Information on Writer Visits and Small Press Materials

Coordinating Council of Literary Magazines, 666 Broadway, New York, NY 10012-2301. (212) 614-6551. Maintains an extensive collection of small literary magazines and publishes an annual catalogue of literary magazines in the United States.

Ferber, E., & Fulton, L. (Eds.). *International Directory of Little Magazines*. Paradise, CA 95969: Dustbooks. Published annually, it lists information on ordering as well as submitting material to small magazines of poetry and fiction.

Poets & Writers, Inc., 201 W. 54th St., New York, NY 10019. (212) 757-1766. Maintains a listing of poets published in its *A Directory of American Poets and Fiction Writers*, including addresses and phone numbers. Shares costs of having listed poets read at public readings throughout the United States.

About the Author

Howard Sage (Ph.D., New York University) is an adjunct associate professor of English as a Second Language at New York University. A former editor of a grant-winning literary journal, *Pulp*, and a poet listed in *A Directory of American Poets and Fiction Writers* (Poets & Writers, Inc.), he has published his poetry in many small press magazines. He is currently working on anthologies of short fiction and poetry for ESL students. His articles have appeared in American Literary Realism, *TESOL Newsletter*, and *English Teaching Forum*. He currently edits the "Miniscules" column of the *TESOL Newsletter* and serves on its editorial board.